CREATING CHANGE THROUGH
FAMILY PHILANTHROPY

CREATING CHANGE THROUGH
FAMILY PHILANTHROPY:
THE NEXT GENERATION

BY ALISON GOLDBERG,
KAREN PITTELMAN
AND RESOURCE GENERATION

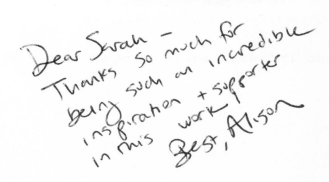

Dear Sarah —
Thanks so much for
being such an incredible
inspiration + supporter
in this work
Best, Alison

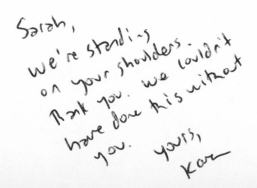

Sarah,
we're standing
on your shoulders.
Thank you. we couldn't
have done this without
you.
yours,
Karen

Book Design by David Janik

Printed in Canada

Published by Soft Skull Press · www.softskull.com
Distributed by Publishers Group West · www.pgw.com · 800.788.3123

Cataloging in Publication is available upon request from the Library of Congress

"Written on gold letters on each of his windows, and on his street level door, too, were these words:

ROSEWATER FOUNDATION
HOW CAN WE HELP
YOU?"

—Kurt Vonnegut

ACKNOWLEDGEMENTS

This book is the result of many people's work. First of all, thank you to the RG staff, both past and present: Sally Bubier, John Harrison, Tracy Hewat, Taij Moteelall, Hez Norton, Jamie Schweser, and Courtney Young. Thanks to the former Foundations for Change consultants, Sarah Feinberg, Lalita Nakarmi, and Aviva Rothman-Shore. Thanks also to everyone who has served on the RG board or volunteered for the organization over the years.

Many thanks to the team who turned our manuscript into a book. Thank you to Richard Nash at Soft Skull Press. Thanks to our editor, John Feffer, and to our copyeditor, Bryn Canner. Thanks to our designer, David Janik.

We are so appreciative of all the interviewees for sharing their stories and insight. Thank you to the amazing interviewers—Eleonora Frey, Cameron Jordan, and Leslie Falconer—for recording these experiences. Thanks also to Michael Kubiak, Nansubuga Mubirumusoke, and Rosalie Prosser for the diligent transcription.

This book would not have been possible without ongoing dialogue about a framework for creating change through family philanthropy. A special thank you to the original Foundations for Change Advisory Board: Peter Diaz, Yee Won Chong, Cheryl Linear, Lily Mendez-Morgan, and Susan Ostrander. Several reviewers took the time to read drafts and provide much helpful advice. Thank you to: Jason Born, Omisade Billie Burney, CJ Callen, Sharna Goldseker, Karen Green, Jeff Krehely, Cameron Jordan, Jonathan Lewis, Laura Loescher, Lily Mendez-Morgan, Susan Price, Lisl Schoepflin, Stephanie Yang, and Prentice Zinn. Thanks also to Kaberi Banerjee and Dennis Delaney at Hemenway & Barnes who provided technical information about trusts, and to Luis Maldonado at the Council on Foundations for interpreting the Pension Protection Act of 2006.

These are just a few of the many other people who've helped shape the ideas in this book: Penny Abeywardena, Calvin Allen, Charlene Allen, Alejandro Amezcua, Kenny Bailey, Christie Balka, Kisha Bird, Amy Bishop, Katrina Browne, Tracy Burt, Patrick Cahn, Mahea Campbell, Armando Castellano, Chuck Collins, Dan Comstock, Oona Coy, Julio Dantas, Alan Davis, Bill Eaton, Nisrin Elamin, Anne Ellinger, Christopher Ellinger, Newell Flather, Tracy Gary, Lisa Gates, Kelin Gersick, Adria Goodson, John Harvey, Jethro Heiko, Rebecca Huston, Maria Jobin-Leeds, Melissa Johnson, Heeten Kalan, Charles Knight, Kalpana Krishnamurthy, Meizhu Lui, Seth Markle, Lydia Morris, Emily Nepon, Mary Phillips, David Perrin, Peter Redington, Rusty Stahl, Alta Starr, Naomi Swinton, Nicole Trombley, John Vaughn, Christian Willauer, and Alicia Wittink.

Thank you to all of the organizations whose work has inspired and informed our own, including: 21/64, Access Strategies Fund, Chahara Foundation, Changemakers, Class Action, Emerging Practioners in Philanthropy, the network of Funding Exchange funds, Joint Affinity Groups, National Network of Grantmakers, People's Institute for Survival and Beyond, Responsible Wealth, Southern Partners Fund, The New World Foundation, Third Wave Foundation, Tides Foundation, United for a Fair Economy, and Western States Center. And to the groups who co-founded RG: Boston Women's Fund, Haymarket People's Fund, More than Money, Peace Development Fund, United Black and Brown Fund, and Youth on Board. A special thank you to the National Committee for Responsive Philanthropy for partnering with RG on book promotion.

Thank you to all the sponsors of this book who've helped support our family philanthropy programs and get this book out into the world: 21/64 a division of Andrea and Charles Bronfman Philanthropies, A. Lindsay and Olive B. O'Connor Foundation, Active Element Foundation, Association of Small Foundations, Boston Women's Fund, Burt Family Foundation, Cameron Jordan, Chahara Foundation, Changemakers, Council on Foundations, Family Legacy Partnership, Ford Foundation, Franklin Weinberg Fund, Funding Exchange, General Service Foundation, Grants Management Associates, Grantmakers Without Borders, Haymarket Peoples Fund, Hill-Snowdon Foundation, Hull Family Foundation, Hunt Alternatives Fund, Nathan Cummings

Foundation, National Network of Grantmakers, The Needmor Fund, Neighborhood Funders Group, Park Foundation, The Philanthropy Workshop, Resist, Inc., Rockefeller Philanthropy Advisors, Ruth and Gerald Dickler Foundation, Simmons Institute for Leadership and Change, Surdna Foundation, Third Wave Foundation, Tides Foundation, United Jewish Communities, W. K. Kellogg Foundation, Women & Philanthropy, and the Young Donor Organizing Alliance.

Alison and Karen would like to thank our families for their love and support. We'd also like to thank Jonathan and Yoav for their never-ending patience. We'll be off the phone in just another minute, we swear . . .

PREFACE

Over the past decade, the philanthropic field has taken a growing interest in what has been termed the "next generation" of family philanthropy. Discussions typically focus on how young people can learn to carry on their family's legacy and leadership. While this book is written for the next generation, it takes a different approach. *Creating Change Through Family Philanthropy* looks at how young people can help transform the field itself.

Founded in 1996, Resource Generation (RG) is a national non-profit organization that works with young people with financial wealth who believe in social change. Led by a cross-class staff and board, RG develops workshops, conferences, and publications that support and challenge its constituents. We have provided programming for over a thousand young people with wealth who want to help create a more just distribution of resources and power.

A few years ago, we began to see a marked increase in the number of young people grappling with their involvement in family philanthropy. Many sensed a conflict between their social change values and the ways their families' funds functioned. They wanted to explore how to participate in family philanthropy while standing by their beliefs. It soon became clear that a new opportunity had emerged for shifting the relationship of family philanthropy to social change.

How could we help young people to question current practices and organize for change within the context of their families' funds? RG began an ongoing dialogue with activists, advisors, academics, and philanthropists to answer this question.[1] Out of these conversations grew the framework for an annual family philanthropy conference, and, eventually, this book.

We believe that if young people are going to succeed in creating lasting change through family philanthropy, they need to look critically at the institution they are inheriting. So while many resource guides focus on lauding philanthropy's benefits, this book looks squarely at its flaws. These chapters investigate how institutional practices within family philanthropy actually perpetuate—rather than ameliorate—inequality.

Creating change also requires young people to confront—and question—the enormous power philanthropy grants their families. This can be a challenge: it's easy to become defensive, to disassociate. Complicated family relationships can mask broader trends, making it harder to see the big picture. And the traditional philanthropic assumption that good intentions automatically lead to good outcomes can forestall a deeper critique.

At RG, we've found that participants can best overcome these hurdles by building an analysis based on their own experiences with privilege. By examining power dynamics in their own family funds, young people can begin to recognize these dynamics on an institutional scale. That's why *Creating Change Through Family Philanthropy* is grounded in the stories of the next generation and draws on firsthand accounts taken from over forty interviews. This approach means that we have focused primarily on young people's experiences with their families' funds as opposed to the experiences of activists and grantees. However, we see our work here as a necessary but solely preliminary step toward creating the meaningful cross-class exchange that true change in philanthropy demands.

This book would certainly not have been possible without the extensive input of activists and social change philanthropy leaders, nor could it exist outside the context of years of innovative work on dismantling racism. It is impossible to understand philanthropic power without understanding its roots in globally interweaving systems of oppression like racism, classism, and sexism. Though we don't intend to collapse these systems into one frame—and we recognize that we can do little more in this space than scratch the surface—we do hope to challenge readers to recognize their privilege in all its forms.

On these pages, we've chosen to avoid certain buzz words like "accountability" and "transparency" that so often pepper critiques of philanthropy. While these words can describe some of the core concepts in this book, their meanings have become diluted from widespread use. Instead, we've attempted to discuss these topics within a more explicit power analysis.

Because it is grounded in an understanding of philanthropy within a particular historical and cultural context, *Creating Change Through Family*

Philanthropy focuses on the United States. We realize that for families in other countries much of what is written here will not apply. We hope, though, that the stories shared will still resonate and serve as a starting point.

Finally, unlike many other philanthropy guides, this book does not articulate a funding agenda. It is not our intention to define funding for social change along specific lines, or to encourage young people with wealth to take this task on. Rather, our hope is that the next generation will imagine a philanthropy that works differently—that they will shift *who* decides what change looks like.

There are now over 33,000 family funds controlling over $209 billion,[2] and most of these funds likely involve a young person in some way. How will the next generation's involvement impact philanthropy? We hope this book will help inspire new directions, both for the hundreds of young people who have been involved in creating change so far and the thousands of others who could join them.

-Alison, Karen, and the RG staff

CONTENTS

SECTION 1

FAMILY PHILANTHROPY
AND SOCIAL CHANGE

INTRODUCTION

It's easy to come up with a list of reasons *not* to get involved in family philanthropy.

We are walking into organizations that were set up, in many cases, before we were even born. We are rarely given an orientation or the necessary information to be effective participants. When meetings are held across the country or in the middle of the week, it's hard to skip school or work to be there. Our family funds[3] may have priorities that we don't agree with. Plus, making decisions as a group of family members certainly isn't the most *efficient* way to give. Agreeing on what to fund—or what to have for lunch—can be a challenge.

On top of all this, family philanthropy grants us power and authority that can feel uncomfortable, or even misplaced. Incredibly experienced non-profit leaders have to prove to us they are deserving of grants. Our funding decisions can make the difference between whether an organization survives or has to shut its doors. Fancy board rooms and fundraisers can make us feel more like we've signed up for a social club then social change. Is this something we really want to be a part of?

Why we need to get involved anyway

On the other hand, there's a big reason why it's *essential* for us to be involved: **As young people who have family funds, we can channel the money and power of family philanthropy toward social justice.**

Collectively family funds control over $209 billion.[4] Yet currently only a tiny percentage of philanthropic resources support social change—one study estimates less than *3 percent* of all foundation giving.[5] As the "next generation," we have the opportunity to dramatically increase that figure.

While the power that comes with getting more involved can feel awkward, it's exactly what makes our involvement imperative. Very few people are given this kind of access. This is our chance to use it for change.

How to get started

Of course, the potential to create change doesn't erase any of the challenges. But with a strong analysis and solid tools, we can be truly effective. This book aims to give you everything you'll need to get started.

First, the focus is on theory. Section 1 begins by exploring how family philanthropy's history shapes the way funds run today and how we can use the concepts of social change philanthropy to frame our analysis. The bulk of the following chapters then examine why family funds' current practices hinder their ability to support social change.

Then it's on to Section 2 and taking action. Because family funds come in different shapes and sizes, you'll get a whole range of strategies. Whether your family's philanthropy is one generation old or five, whether the giving is in the thousands or the millions, there are many steps you can take.

The language of family philanthropy can be a confusing one filled with complicated jargon, mysterious acronyms, and strange terminology derived from tax code. If you're ever feeling lost, the Appendix has definitions, rules, and explanations.

What is social change?

There isn't just one definition of social change. Social change encompasses many different issues from affordable housing to equal participation in the political process, from immigrant rights to dismantling racism. As a result, individuals and groups that are working for social change have many different visions for a better world. A common thread, though, is that social change activists address the *systems* that are creating inequalities rather than only ameliorating the symptoms.[6]

At RG, we define social change broadly to mean **creating a more just distribution of power and resources**. Currently, the top 10 percent of wealth holders in the United States have 70 percent of the wealth.[7] The world's wealthiest 500 individuals have a combined income greater than that of the poorest 416 million people.[8] These statistics don't require a lot of interpretation to demonstrate that the current state of affairs is unjust.

Creating change through family philanthropy requires tackling some difficult topics: money, power, privilege, politics, communication across generations, establishing respectful collaborations. But you don't need to take this on all alone. As you'll see in the stories shared throughout the book, there's a growing community of young people who are supporting and challenging each other to do this work.

Getting involved

"I am motivated by learning about causes that interest me and the chance to support great projects that are not getting funds from the government or other foundations."   **-Patrick, 22**

"I'm fascinated and excited by social justice organizing and making the world the most beautiful place that it can be for the largest amount of people possible. Having access to money is a tool that can help me to do that."   **-Jamie, 32**

"I think part of my motivation is coming from having so much privilege and realizing how unfair that is."   **-Rachel, 27**

"Due to the structure of the economy and the tax system, my family has accumulated wealth at a direct expense to society. I have inherited financial resources, and my response is to redistribute wealth. Commitment to social justice guides where those resources go."   **-Holmes, 29**

"What has been important to me about our family philanthropy is that it's not just about giving money away, but being able to do this together as a family and working through the conflicts that we have. And, really celebrating the fact that we have three generations coming together to do this."   **-Hopie, 23**

CHAPTER 1: PHILANTHROPY FOR WEALTHY FAMILIES

The word "philanthropy" is often used as a synonym for giving or generosity.[9] By that definition, family philanthropy means families giving together in all forms: volunteering for a soup kitchen, writing a check to a community organization, caring for a relative . . . Families from all backgrounds share time and resources in many different ways.

But the "family philanthropy" we're looking at here is something different. It doesn't include all forms of giving, and it doesn't apply to all families that give. Instead, this family philanthropy is an exclusive institution in the United States that's made up of foundations, donor-advised funds, and charitable trusts.

What is an institution?

An institution is an organization or a system of organizations. Banks, hospitals, and schools are just a few examples. Institutional policies evolve over time, shaping rules, practices, and cultural norms. An institution has a force that's all its own—its agendas and influence hold a greater collective power than that of any of the individuals involved.

Family philanthropy is exclusionary

Access to the institution of family philanthropy is restricted to those with significant wealth. Setting up a foundation entails steep legal and accounting expenses, in addition to assets for giving—some estimate that $1 million is the minimum amount required.[10] While donor-advised funds and charitable trusts can be created with less, family philanthropy organizations and events are, by and large, limited to participants granting tens of thousands of dollars a year.[11]

Why is the institution of family philanthropy so restrictive? To understand this, we'll have to look at its history.[12]

Family philanthropy began in the Industrial Revolution

Foundations were established as legal entities in the early 1800s, but wealthy families didn't begin using these vehicles for philanthropy until the end of that century. Spurred by the mounting concentration of private wealth during the Industrial Revolution and the introduction of the federal income and estate taxes, a growing number of donors set up funds as mechanisms to shelter their assets.

By creating foundations, wealthy families received more than major tax relief.[13] They were able to pay family members high salaries. Families could use their foundations as investment partners by placing their funds' assets in companies where they had a vested interest. Until 1969, foundations weren't even required to give any money away.

The early family foundations also played a considerable public relations role. In an era when 10 percent of the population controlled 90 percent of the wealth,[14] powerful businessmen used their foundations' giving to recast their role from profiteers to benefactors. Industrialists like John D. Rockefeller and Andrew Carnegie sponsored spectacular public works, making a show of supporting the common good. Yet the social and economic conditions their charity addressed were often caused directly by their own business practices.[15]

Family philanthropy today

Since these early years the institution of family philanthropy has mushroomed. There are now over 33,000 family foundations, thousands of philanthropic trusts and donor-advised funds, and an extensive network of supporting organizations. The impact of family fund giving is highly visible everywhere, from libraries to universities to hospitals.

The Tax Reform Act of 1969 introduced some significant changes in the field. For example, the Act required foundations to spend at least 5 percent of their assets each year and regulated investment practice. More recently, the Pension Protection Act of 2006 restricted how donor-advised funds can be used.[16] Still, family philanthropy continues to serve as a way for the wealthy to concentrate money, power, and control across generations.

Philanthropic assets are public resources. By contributing to a family fund, a donor receives tax deductions. The fund is then legally bound to distribute that money to the public for charitable purposes.[17] Yet family philanthropy is structured so that the public has no say in how resources are allocated. The power remains with the donors and their descendants. Because there are no limits on how long foundations can exist or how large they can become, this power can then be passed onto successive generations indefinitely.

If we want to use family philanthropy for social change, we can't lose sight of where the institution came from. Its history influences everything: how much we give, the ways we give, even why we find ourselves in positions of authority. We can't change the past. But we can challenge it—and help change family philanthropy's future.

What gets in our way

"I never really knew that there was any money, or what a foundation was. At sixteen, my father invited me to join the next generation advisory committee. I came to meetings, but I was completely in the dark about how the foundation worked. And nobody really took the time to explain it to me." -Eleonora, 29

"When you don't know anything about foundations, how they work can be really intimidating. For at least three years I just observed and listened so I could understand the workings of the foundation and how grants were made." -Zoe, 26

"Unlike the members of my parent's generation who have flexible work schedules and are primarily based in Michigan, the members of my generation are all over the place and have to work around school vacations and things like that to even come to meetings." -Mary, 34

"It's really hard to work with family. My mom calls me and I never just hear, 'Hi, how are you? How is life?' She always jumps right into talking about the work that we are doing together. How can we work together with our families but still keep family separate from the work?" -Chloe, 29

"I think the biggest questions I grapple with are, 'What does it mean to be a funder *and* someone who works for the non-profit field? How can I justify taking a job in the non-profit field when I don't need the income and so many people do?'" -Rachel, 27

"An inner struggle that I've had my whole life is coming to terms with the world that I live in and the reality that the other 99 percent of the world doesn't have the same wealth." -Maura, 31

"It was a challenge at first to actually get over the fact that I had the privilege of giving away money. In fact, the first year I only sponsored one grant and that was with a lot of arm-twisting. Just being in the position to give away money and how that feels . . . especially when working with groups that are advocating for a more fair and just society. How do I fit into that by having this money? Is giving a grant really going to change that? Am I just part of the problem?" -Mindy, 25

CHAPTER 2: PHILANTHROPY FOR SOCIAL CHANGE

Family philanthropy wasn't established to redistribute resources. Yet, throughout the past century a small number of families have found ways to use their funds to support social change. If we want to transform our own family funds, we'll need to draw from that history. We'll also need to explore an alternative framework for giving: social change philanthropy.

What is social change philanthropy?

Social change philanthropy has its roots in the movements of the 1960s.[18] During that time, donors and activists began creating new public foundations[19] that reflected the values of the era's struggles for peace, women's rights, and racial justice. Some of the earliest examples of these new funds included the Brotherhood Crusade, an African-American community fund, and Resist, a foundation created to support war resisters and student organizing.

Since its inception, social change philanthropy has been a vital strategy for funding issues of equity and justice. This success is due in large part to a focus on democratizing the giving process. Social change philanthropy puts decision-making power into the hands of activists and community members, not just wealthy donors. As a result, funds have the experience necessary to respond more effectively to movements' shifting needs. By tying the principles of social change to philanthropic practice, this philosophy challenges funds to reflect their mission in everything from day-to-day operations to investment policy.

Over the past thirty-five years, many different groups, from workplace-giving federations to private foundations, have adopted these ideas. There are now close to 200 activist-led funds focused on a wide range of geographic regions, population groups, and issue areas around the world.[20]

Family philanthropy has a history of supporting social change

There's also a tradition of family funds supporting social change that stretches back almost one hundred years. The Julius Rosenwald Foundation, established in 1917, gave grants to organizations like the Highlander Center, an important training ground for union organizers in the South.[21] The Wieboldt Foundation was founded in 1921 in the hope that its grants would assist "charities designed to put an end to the need for charity."[22] The foundation aided the launch of the Mexican-American civil rights organization that became the United Farm Workers Union.[23]

More recently, a few family foundations have sought to address inequality not only through their giving but also the ways they give. Funds like the General Service Foundation and The Needmor Fund have adopted the principles of social change philanthropy by including both activists and family members on their boards.[24] Other family funds have transferred decision-making power entirely to activists. The New World Foundation embarked on a process to phase out family involvement and become a public fund.[25] The Bert and Mary Meyer Foundation turned its assets over to grantees to create a new activist-led organization, the Southern Partners Fund.[26]

Building the tradition

Family funds *can* support social change: foundations like these have proven it. But to truly build on their tradition, we'll need more than history. A strong analysis of current practices in the field is an essential tool. By drawing on the concepts of social change philanthropy, we can shape a deeper critique. The next chapter begins the process with the fundamental question: Where does the money go?

Philanthropy across generations

"It has been a growing experience to be able to sit down around a table with twelve fifty-year-old well-established businessmen and doctors and just speak my mind and be able to compose my thoughts."   -Dan, 25

"When a lot of the younger generation came on the board, I think some older family members were really scared that we were going to bring down the integrity or reputation of the foundation. They created an application process which had questions like, 'Why is it important to give grants?' And, 'Why is it good to help people?' They also made a stipulation that new, young grantmakers had to go to some kind of conference on grantmaking. This felt like a double standard since not one of the older generation members had to go through any application or training process."   -Rachel, 27

"Some of the staff and family members can be patronizing and have an exaggerated idea of the different perspective that young people bring."   -Patrick, 22

"I feel very respected at the table and that people actually value my comments, especially because a lot of the work [we fund] has to do with young people. When I initially got involved my connection was relating everything to my friends and people my age and how they would be affected."   -Zoe, 26

"As a young person, I have a multi-issue approach, especially regarding diversity and identity. I value youth-run and youth-led organizations."   -Tracy, 35

"I think substantially more about the environment because I was born at a time when all major systems of the earth needed for the survival of our species are in great jeopardy."   -David, 25

13

CHAPTER 3: WHERE DOES THE MONEY GO?

Despite the seemingly infinite variety of funds' grantmaking interests, family philanthropy giving tends to concentrate in three areas: education (in particular colleges and universities), arts and culture, and human services.[27] There's also a pattern to what family philanthropy *doesn't* fund. **Only a marginal amount of money goes to communities that experience inequality and discrimination.**[28]

Family philanthropy is not redistributing resources

An incredibly small percentage of family philanthropy's resources and foundation resources overall are supporting low-income people; people of color; indigenous peoples; immigrants and refugees; international communities; lesbian, gay, bisexual and transgender people (LGBT); and women and girls.

For example, in 2004, only 7.6 percent of all large foundation grant dollars went to communities of color, and only 5.2 percent went to women and girls organizations. Immigrant and refugee organizations received only 0.9 percent of the funding, and LGBT organizations received just 0.2 percent.[29] While the statistics are inconclusive about the exact amount that goes to low-income communities, it's minimal.[30]

Why is this happening? While there are many possible reasons for the trend, *who* is making decisions in family philanthropy has a big influence on *what* gets funded.

Who makes the decisions?

From the earliest funds to the present-day, donors have commonly appointed their own family members as decision makers. Because the institution of family philanthropy itself is restricted to people with wealth, the majority of grantmakers come from privileged families and don't experience significant economic hardship.

At the same time, people of color rarely lead family philanthropy. This is due in large part to the racial wealth divide—the gap in wealth between families of color and white families. For example, in 2001, the median net worth of families of color was only $17,100 compared to $120,900 for white families.[31] Currently, only 2.2 percent of family foundation trustees are people of color.[32] Almost everyone at the family philanthropy decision-making table is wealthy and white.

How does this affect what gets funded?

In the institution of family philanthropy, funding priorities derive primarily from donors' personal interests and networks.[33] Philanthropists often focus on organizations that have touched their lives, whether it's giving back to an alma mater or sponsoring the local symphony. They also tend to fund groups that people in their networks are involved with and currently supporting. Many donors look to personal connections to confer legitimacy.

When privileged experiences and networks shape where the money goes, the bulk of funding is directed to wealthy, white communities and concerns. We also can't forget that, no matter how charitable the intentions, wealthy families have a vested interest in maintaining the status quo.[34] As a result, supporting communities that experience inequality and discrimination is a low priority in the field.

What about funds that do support social change?

Even when family funds do commit to supporting social change, the seats at the decision-making table remain reserved for relatives. Community members and movement leaders are seldom invited in and their absence significantly impairs the process. Grantmaking choices continue to be characterized by family networks and connections. Without activist expertise, families are also ill-equipped to assess an organization's long-term potential and overall movement strategy.

Here's a quick example: A family fund wants to address widespread asthma caused by air pollution in a local low-income community. The family decides to support a hospital clinic run by a well-known doctor. But without consulting activists and residents, family members are not aware of an upcoming parent-led health fair. They miss the importance of a grassroots campaign pressuring government officials to upgrade a nearby bus depot—one of the primary sources of the pollution. And family members overlook activists who are reframing the problem entirely by pointing to the need for local political representation. Lacking these perspectives, the fund's grantmaking is considerably less effective.

Perhaps most importantly, family funds are denying people a voice in decisions about significant resources that are affecting their lives. In this way, funders wind up further marginalizing the very communities they mean to empower. Even if family members bring their own experiences with inequality and discrimination to the table, broader representation beyond family is still essential. As long as decision-making authority is based solely on proximity to wealth, family philanthropy will be unable to truly support social change.

Shifting power

Proposing a more democratic decision-making process can inspire a lot of resistance. Many families fear that this will mean the end of their own involvement. Some do not see a value in activist and community member expertise and trust only in privileged credentials and degrees. Others assume that people outside the family will have no interest and that efforts to involve them are a waste of time and money. It will also take much more than just inviting in new decision makers to ensure their voices are heard. Until tokenism,[35] entrenched power dynamics, and family assumptions about race and class are addressed, real change can't occur.

These are only a few of the reasons why opening up our funds' decision-making processes can feel like a monumental task. Yet the fact remains that family philanthropy's assets are public resources, not private property. Even if we succeed in moving more grant money to social change, as long as the real power over these resources rests only with those who are wealthy and white, how much has really changed? Questioning how power is held in family philanthropy has the potential to completely transform our funds—and the field.

Access Strategies Fund (ASF) is a family foundation that was created in 1999. It was established to support community-based organizations in Massachusetts working with disenfranchised communities involved in the democratic process. ASF supports these groups in their efforts to increase and leverage electoral participation to advance more responsive public policies.

ASF is a great example of a family foundation that has brought community representation and social change expertise into multiple layers of its grantmaking and governance. Since its inception seven years ago, ASF has taken a number of steps to open up its decision-making process, described in the timeline below. This evolution has taken place through many conversations between family members, community activists, and non-family staff spanning several years. ASF continues on a path toward more inclusive grantmaking to support its social change strategies and goals.

1999

ASF is incorporated as a private foundation with the original donor couple sitting on the board.

One of the donors becomes the executive director. She meets with community activists, elected officials, community leaders, and academics to help inform the focus of the foundation.

During its first year of operation, ASF makes grants with the guidance of a local activist-led foundation.

2000-2001

A director of grantmaking is hired—a woman of color who has experience in state-level legislative politics and community-based organizational management.

A diverse group of community activists is convened to help develop the mission statement and funding guidelines.

The foundation launches an annual event for all grantees to network with each other and participate in a capacity-building program. In the first year, the Alliance for Justice leads a workshop on the lobbying rules for non-profit organizations.

2002-2003

The grantmaking guidelines become public and ASF launches a website.

The grantmaking committee is created to represent geographic, ethnic, age, and class diversity. The committee reviews all proposals and makes recommendations to the staff and board. Committee members are compensated for their expertise and time at comparable rates to other professional consultants.

2004-2006

Because the roster of grantees becomes relatively stable, foundation staff and board are able to spend time leveraging other funds for their partners. Also, referrals are made when foundation colleagues are looking for staff or consultants from the communities the foundation supports.

The family board promotes the director of grantmaking to the position of executive director.

The board of directors is expanded to include a member outside the family with community expertise.

Decision-making power

"There are sibling and parent and child relationships and they all come into the family foundation board room. It's not just business when we get into making philanthropy decisions—it's a lot about family history and legacy issues and all the dynamics that go on."

-Mary, 34

"The issues surrounding why we have the power to give away this money—and that the final decision of who will receive the money which we give away is based entirely on our values and life experiences—has never been brought up in a foundation meeting."

-David, 30

"There just really isn't much diversity among the trustees. So this year we are trying to increase our diversity to bring different perspectives to an all-white family."

-Rachel, 27

"I've often posed this question at the foundation: Am I the most qualified person to serve on a board or is there somebody more qualified? Does being a family member give me the right to be on it or should it be something that's earned because of what I've done, how I've been involved, and my knowledge of the issues?"

-Ridgway, 25

"I joined the staff of a non-profit organization as their grantwriter because I am familiar with the world of philanthropy. I think that I understand the way foundation board members' minds work. I understand what they're looking for since I have sat through hours and hours of conversations at board meetings. I know how relational it is. I know how important it is for grantees to directly address the intentions of the foundation, to speak their language. And I know how whimsical boards are and how quickly they can change their minds based on someone's feelings at that moment."

-Maura, 31

CHAPTER 4: HOW ARE GRANTS MADE?

The grantmaking process is defined as all the steps a fund goes through to solicit, assess, and respond to requests for money. An imbalanced power dynamic is inherent in this process: the fund controls resources that organizations require. However, rather than mitigating this imbalance, many current practices in family philanthropy actually magnify it.

The process is tailored to funders' needs

Many family funds share only the barest minimum of information about themselves. With no website, contact information, or publicly available guidelines, funds send organizations on a wild goose chase just to learn how to apply.

And that's just the beginning. Funders often request a huge amount of information from prospective grantees: extensive narratives, elaborate budgets, exhaustive outcome measures. Yet they hardly ever consider if what they're asking of organizations is reasonable in relation to the resources offered. Proposals can run upwards of twenty pages and the process can demand hundreds of hours—and thousands of dollars of staff time. In the end, the odds of receiving a grant are low. Moreover, almost every family has their own unique application, which means organizations have to start all over again for each new fund they approach.

Smaller grassroots groups seldom have the capacity to embark on this process. As a result, larger, established organizations with more fundraising resources dominate family philanthropy's applicant pool.

The entire grantmaking process is tailored to the needs of funders. From timing to location to even the simplest communications, everything is structured around preferences of family, staff, and board. As a result, the thirty-three thousand-plus family funds in this country are all over the map in terms of what they ask for and when they want it.

Lack of operating support

Funders often assume that an efficient organization spends most of its money on program expenses while keeping administrative costs minimal. For this reason, family funds rarely provide general operating support and may look suspiciously at groups with anything more than a bare bones administrative budget.[36] The truth is, organizations need money to pay for rent, salaries, supplies, technology, printing, and all the other components of a smoothly running office. A program grant is meaningless if an organization can't afford to keep the lights on.[37]

Strings attached

Funders continue to set the agenda, even after a grant is made. Time-consuming evaluation reports are a common requirement and typically ignore how organizations assess their own progress. Participating in funder-driven collaborations and trainings is often mandatory, whether or not this aligns with grantees' own priorities. Evaluation, collaboration, and training are real organizational needs. But these needs can't be met effectively without grantee input.

Fear of commitment

Many funders restrict their grants to a maximum of 2-3 years, which means their giving often ends just when a group starts to succeed. Social change is difficult and slow—it can take years to establish a new program. Yet, funders act as temporary investors with no stake in long-term success, forcing organizations to continually seek new support.

We're on the same side

Family philanthropy's grantmaking process is characterized by a lack of communication and trust. Funders assume the sole prerogative to set the rules of a game where grantees are treated like the opposing team. But when it comes to social change, shouldn't we all be on the same side? Philanthropists may provide money, but it's the energy and commitment of activists that makes the work happen.

If we want to truly join forces, we'll need to tear down the walls around our funds that block communication. While it may seem like those walls protect us—both as funders and as people with wealth— they actually compromise our effectiveness. A responsive and respectful grantmaking process would make us all more successful in creating change.

Thoughts from Activists on Grantmaking

These comments come from years of ongoing dialogue at Resource Generation.

- Listen to organizations and movements about what sustainable and effective funding means and develop giving strategies accordingly.

- Don't make organizations jump through hoops that require lots of time in the grant application process. Be respectful of organizations' time.

- Be clear about your intentions and expectations.

- Think about ways you can learn about organizations and communities outside the proposal process.

- Use funding to encourage collaboration, not competition, among your potential grantees.

- Use an anti-oppression lens in your giving and articulate your commitment as a funder to addressing oppression. Focus on how family philanthropy can address the root causes of racism, sexism, and homophobia.

- Involve people who are most affected by injustice to support social change. It's the only way to ensure consistent questioning of the status quo.

- Give multi-year, unrestricted funding.

- Give grants on a rolling basis and provide emergency support.

- Make funding available for organizing, training, infrastructure development, and cross-sectoral approaches.

- Fund organizations led by people of color and pay attention to culture. Be aware that one size does not fit all.

- Share your understanding about how philanthropy works and partner with organizations to change how philanthropy is structured.

- Talk with the groups you are giving money to about how you can help with fundraising. Connect grantees to other funders.

- Use your access and connections with organizations and people who hold power to raise awareness about the issues.

- Work with organizations to set funding goals and develop evaluation methods. Both you and the organization want maximum impact, but the organization needs to define what the impact looks like and how to measure it. If you want reflection and evaluation, include that in your funding.

Advice on getting involved

"Don't be hard on yourself at first because it can be a daunting task to simply begin to get involved in your family's philanthropy."

-David, 25

"Ask lots of questions of other members. Become friends with foundation staff."

-Rebecca, 25

"Get connected to people who are doing the work, ask questions, and don't be afraid to get out there."

-Andy, 27

"Find yourself a really good mentor who believes in you and supports you, and who is not your mother."

-Mindy, 25

"Educate yourself about the issues. Develop close relationships with grantees, especially the ones doing really great work that you are going to fund year in and year out, and talk to them about who they see doing important work. This can get political, but it can also be really valuable."

-Melanie, 30

"Build a network of people who can be a resource for you and that you can count on as advisors. Seek opportunities to be a part of a group of people who have similar issues and concerns."

-Maria, 36

"As a family member it is highly unlikely that you will be fired. Do not be afraid to back a project that others may consider risky."

-Patrick, 22

"Do your research. Find out about the history of the foundation and how decisions are made. Read all the documentation you can. Go to trainings and decide how you would like to be involved. The potential to move money and engage in social change dialogue with your family is huge."

-Tracy, 35

CHAPTER 5: WHERE THE REST OF THE MONEY GOES

In 2004, family foundations had $209 billion in assets, but gave only $12.7 billion away.[38] That's a mere 6 percent. Grantmaking may be family philanthropy's most visible activity, but the vast majority of its resources remain in investments.

Funds focus on growth

The laws and policies that guide family philanthropy actually encourage a focus on investing over giving. Funds are required to grant only a minimal percentage of their assets—private foundations have a required annual distribution of 5 percent—and are taxed at a very low rate.[39]

The link between investing and grantmaking is seldom made.[40] Family funds often invest in companies that bring high returns but directly contradict their grantmaking missions. For example, it's not uncommon for a foundation to support environmental groups while at the same time holding shares in companies that are major polluters. Luckily, there is a whole field of investing that specializes in dealing with this conflict.

What is SRI?

Socially Responsible Investing (SRI)[41] takes more than just profit into account. SRI also uses social and ethical criteria to guide the investment process. Over the past thirty years, SRI has grown to include a number of methods that can help funds align their investments with their mission.

SCREENING means creating a set of guidelines to specify what types of companies to invest in or avoid. For example, a fund that focuses on human rights could screen out companies that use sweat-shop labor and seek out companies that have livable wage policies.

In COMMUNITY INVESTING, a fund supports alternative financial institutions that then direct resources toward low- and middle-income communities. Examples include providing below-market-rate loans for affordable housing and small business development.

SHAREHOLDER ACTIVISM involves influencing corporate practices from within. This can include actively voting proxies,[42] joining together with other shareholders to file resolutions, and opening a direct dialogue with corporate management. For example, a foundation concerned with deforestation could introduce a shareholder resolution banning the purchase of wood from old-growth forests.

SRI and family philanthropy

A small number of funds have taken the lead on bringing SRI to family philanthropy.[43] The directors of the Weeden Foundation decided to "reduce the dissonance between the foundation's mission and investment strategies" by engaging in shareholder activism, investment screening, and program-related investments.[44] The Nathan Cummings Foundation created a proxy voting policy that states it will always vote for the benefit of its grantmaking programs and submit shareholder resolutions to create change.[45] The Jessie Smith Noyes Foundation has also taken numerous steps to leverage its assets for social change: comprehensively screening all investments, filing shareholder resolutions in collaboration with a grantee, and writing letters to companies where it owns shares.[46]

Currently, though, SRI's tools are vastly underused in the field. One survey found that only 20 percent of family foundations do any kind of social screening with respect to investments.[47] Another survey showed that less than 9 percent of foundations had any written guidelines for voting proxies.[48] It's also extremely rare for funds to consult with grantees about investments or file shareholder resolutions together, despite the potential power of such collaborations.

Investing is an integral part of philanthropy

Many families fear switching to SRI will mean earning lower returns. However, several studies have demonstrated that socially responsible funds perform competitively.[49] While making a detailed case for change can be complicated, especially with larger foundations, the evidence and expertise we'll need is readily accessible.

We don't have to undermine our grantmaking to grow our endowments. The truth is, when almost the entirety of family philanthropy's assets are kept in investments, we can't afford to. Investing may turn out to have the greatest impact of all. We have to help make it an integral part of philanthropy.

What will success look like?

"In the future, success to me would look like a broader group of voices making decisions and investments that match our values more fully." **-Oona, 29**

"My vision is to engage in a process of social change with my family, to move money to organizations that are working for change by addressing root causes, and to meet the responsibility I feel for using my privilege to create positive social change." **-Tracy, 35**

"In the short term, I'd like to see the LGBT work we fund become more grassroots-focused rather than giving to the larger national organizations first and foremost. And I want to be more involved in making the funding more strategic." **-Jonathan, 24**

"The resources would be fully committed to one or more public foundations with a transparent and accountable process for supporting direct action organizations committed to social justice." **-Holmes, 29**

"I have great hopes for better leadership and better organization among progressive family foundations. I feel like there's a great opportunity for family funders who are already involved in progressive philanthropy to make a strategic case to other foundations." **-Ashley, 29**

"Ideally the foundation can eventually dissolve with all the money having been used for the purposes it was intended, and society can internalize all costs in a manner that eliminates the need for philanthropy in the first place." **-David, 25**

CHAPTER 6: HOW LONG WILL FAMILY PHILANTHROPY EXIST?

Many family funds are established "in perpetuity," which means they are created to exist forever. In the field, it's a given that most families will want their philanthropy to go on indefinitely. But is this really the best strategy for creating change?

Why create a fund that lasts forever?

The reason why most funds are established in perpetuity has more to do with estate planning than grantmaking. Estate planning is the process of determining how a person's resources should be distributed after death. A whole professional estate planning industry exists and its standard priority is to help individuals preserve wealth while avoiding taxes. Because foundations and trusts are effective vehicles for transferring assets to descendants and offer significant tax benefits, estate planners often encourage people with wealth to make use of them.

When a fund is created primarily to preserve wealth for multiple generations, setting it up for long-term growth makes sense. Estate planning also places a high value on the idea of upholding legacy. Here, too, perpetuity is the obvious option: an enduring family fund ensures that descendants will represent the donor's values for years to come.

Family philanthropy is passed on across generations

Subsequent generations also have a choice about whether or not to continue the family's philanthropy. Since they are in charge of governance, family members could still decide to give away more money in a shorter period of time. However, the default practice in most families is to keep "payout"—the percentage of assets spent—at a minimum, so that funds will grow for the future. This is because the donor's descendants benefit from perpetuity, too.

Family funds provide members with the opportunity to become major contributors to issues they care about. Retaining authority over philanthropic resources becomes a considerable incentive for keeping payout low. Families also benefit from using their funds as a tool to teach their children about philanthropy. Many view a family fund as a valuable way to help the next generation learn about generosity and giving.

Mission is missing from payout decisions

The Aaron Diamond Foundation, a fund dedicated to supporting HIV/AIDS prevention, is a rare example of a family foundation that based its payout decisions on its mission. Recognizing HIV/AIDS as a massive and urgent problem, the fund chose to give the entirety of its $220 million away in just ten years. The result was a series of grants with considerable impact. For instance, The Aaron Diamond AIDS Research Center, founded in 1991 with a major grant from the foundation, helped to develop the combination drug therapy that has dramatically reduced the death rate from AIDS in the United States.[50]

Perpetuity in and of itself isn't wrong. In fact, it can be an important strategy for building permanent social change resources.[51] But other strategies exist as well, like spending down, transferring the principal to grantees, and merging assets with activist-led funds. The problem is that perpetuity is the unchallenged norm for all of family philanthropy, and that mission is left out of payout decisions altogether.

A new legacy

Where is the line between giving as a family and maintaining generations-long control? How much money should a fund hold onto and how much should be given away? These questions are essential if we want to use our funds to support social change. To ask them, though, demands we question perpetuity.

As the next generation, we can help take the lead. After all, when funds are set up in perpetuity, they are growing for our benefit. We are the ones who receive the advantage when we participate in funder-only conversations, introduce our own children to a family foundation, or inherit income from a charitable remainder trust. We can call for a different kind of legacy: a commitment to supporting social change today.

Philanthropic power

"I moved to Michigan to learn more about the foundation and the community where it is based. Since I've been there, I often get asked if I am part of my family's foundation. Everyone knows my last name. It allows me to meet with people that I shouldn't be able to meet with as a person who has never lived in this community, as a person in her mid-twenties. There's an instant recognition attached to being a part of a large foundation." **-Eleonora, 29**

"I'm getting benefits that go beyond the family foundation itself. It is also a personal springboard to get involved in the wider field of philanthropy in a way that I couldn't if I didn't have some role within my own family foundation. It's like the key to entry in a different world that otherwise you're not allowed in." **-Christopher, 25**

"I think that a lot of things that are associated with privilege are things that I value. It's great to be able to call people up on the phone who know a lot about a subject and ask them to talk to you about it. Those kinds of networks and connections are great. I just think more people should have them." **-Maria, 36**

"A lot of times I was really turned off because I felt like program officers at great big foundations were up in an ivory tower and almost condescending to the people they were making grants to. I wanted to be much closer to our grantees. But then as soon as somebody finds out you have access to capital, it's like, 'I have this friend who's heading this organization and there's this organization and there's this organization . . .' That's really awkward as well." **-Melanie, 30**

"My dad's brother is the president of the foundation. I don't see myself doing that. Your name becomes synonymous with money." **-Dan, 25**

"A representative from one of the local universities took me to lunch. He asked me, 'Do you find people treat you differently when they know who you are?' And I wanted to say to him, 'Would you take another program assistant to lunch?' But instead I said, 'It depends. If it's a grantee, it's inherently skewed. There is a person who wants something and a person who has power to give it. Someone who puts what they really care about on the line is going to do whatever they can to get funding, and rightly so.' It's a tough issue and I don't think you ever really get to overcome it. I think it's just accepting that this is the role I have to play, and I have to do the best I can not to get sucked up into it."   -Ridgway, 25

SECTION 2

TAKING ACTION

INTRODUCTION TO THE TAKING ACTION SECTION

Until now, we've been looking at the theory behind creating change through family philanthropy. Now it's time for some practice. In the pages that follow you'll find resources to help you assess, strategize, start dialogue, and take concrete action. Of course, every family fund's path to change will be different, but this section can give you the tools you'll need to chart your course.

Since social change is new territory for many family funds, these chapters focus on first steps: making proposals, navigating resistances, building consensus. For some families that may seem daunting. Other families have a lot more experience. Feel free to skip around. To cut and paste. To use what makes sense now and put aside what may make sense for later.

A number of chapters focus predominantly on assessment and consist of in-depth lists of questions. These assessments can help you compile key information and tackle tough issues of power and philanthropy. The chapters also offer reflection exercises that examine the intersection between how we feel and how funds operate.

The bulk of Section 2 addresses how to shift the funding process from every angle: what gets funded, how it happens, who decides. It also looks at the assets that aren't distributed and how to move these to socially responsible investments. Finally, it explores taking on the taboo topic of whether or not our funds should even hold onto these assets.

Keep in mind that while the chapter order may suggest each action must follow one after another, this is far from true. All of these topics are interconnected. New voices at the table may mean new funding priorities. A shift in funding priorities may lead to new voices at the table. Grantmaking, investing, and payout are all inextricably linked—every change you make will determine the terms of your next step.

Doing this work with our families isn't easy, but even when you hit an impasse, you have options. Chapter 8 offers suggestions on how to improve family communication and move forward. There are also many steps you can take on your own. For example, Chapter 17 looks at ways we can use the power family philanthropy grants us to create change within the institution itself.

When you're ready to dive in, Chapter 18 will guide you through writing an action plan. If you're looking for inspiration, throughout Section 2 you'll find profiles of young people in family philanthropy reflecting on what their paths have been and what lies ahead. Because there are also many other helpful publications and organizations, every chapter will point you toward the Resource Section.

The trick to all of this is to start where your family is starting—to figure out when to challenge and when to compromise. Remember that this is about getting resources out there and that even the smallest shifts can still lead to lasting change.

CHAPTER 7: ASSESS WHERE YOU'RE STARTING

Figuring out what you know—and what you need to know—is the crucial first step for creating change. Once you understand where you're starting from you can begin tailoring your tactics.

ASSESSMENT

PART 1: WHO IS INVOLVED?
Official board members and trustees aren't the only ones who control the way a family fund runs. From staff to advisors to heavily influential friends, the list of those involved can be quite long. The chart below can help you keep track. Don't forget to include professionals like estate planners, accountants, and lawyers.

WHO:	ROLE(S):

PART 2: HOW IS THE FUND RUN?

History

Who decided to start the family fund? When? Why?

Where did the money come from?

Does the fund have a mission statement?

Is it a foundation, donor-advised fund, charitable trust, or something else? (See the Appendix for definitions.) Why was this particular structure chosen?

If the family gives through multiple funds, how are they different from one another?

How has the fund changed over time? Who have been the major players in shaping that change? Have non-family members played a role?

Assets

How much money is currently in the fund? How is it invested?

Is money still being contributed to the fund (donations, estate gifts, trust distributions)?

What is the long-term plan for the fund? How will leadership transition? Is it set up to exist in perpetuity or to pay out the assets?

Is there a budget? What does it include?

Management

Where is the fund based? Is there an office?

Is the fund housed within another institution? Why was that institution chosen?

How is the fund run? Is there a staff? Is there a board? Are there committees?

What does staff, board, and consultant compensation look like? How does this compare to other funds?[52]

How are meetings run? Is there a formal protocol, like Roberts Rules of Order, or is it more free-form?

How do members make decisions? Is there a formal process?

How do members bring new ideas to the table?

Who is eligible to participate in the fund?

How are new members brought in?

How do young people participate? Is there a next generation board or fund?

How does the fund evaluate itself? How often?

Giving

How much money is given away each year?

What issues and/or communities does the fund support? Are there "program areas"?

Key documents for your files

- Mission statement
- Founding documents such as foundation articles of incorporation and bylaws, trust documents, or donor-advised fund agreements
- Tax returns: IRS Forms 990 PF and 1023 (for foundations); IRS Forms 1041, 1041-A, and 5227 (for trusts)
- Budgets
- Recent financial statements
- Annual reports
- Minutes
- Any policy documents (e.g., conflict-of-interest, investment policy)
- Grantmaking documents (See Chapter 11 for a detailed list.)

If there is a grantmaking focus, why was it chosen? What was the process for deciding it? Who was involved?

Are certain organizations regularly supported?

If the fund is a trust, who are the charitable and non-charitable beneficiaries?

How are grantmaking decisions made? Who makes them?

Do board or family members have access to discretionary funds?

PART 3: ASSESS YOUR INFLUENCE[53]

Mark the scale for each of the following questions. The more your answers fall to the right, the greater your current influence in your family fund may be. Keeping this in mind will help you create a realistic action plan.

How long have you been involved in your family fund?
Not involved yet ⬅———————————➡ Old-timer

How involved have you been?
A little ⬅———————————➡ A lot

Do you feel like your participation in the fund is valued by other members?
Not so much ⬅———————————➡ Highly

What's your relationship like with the family?
Not so close ⬅———————————➡ Couldn't be closer

How does your family fund feel about next generation involvement?
Resistant ⬅———————————➡ Supportive

How do your political views compare to other fund members' views?
In the minority ⬅———————————➡ In the majority

Do you feel like your vision of social change is respected?
No ⬅———————————➡ Yes

How would you describe communication among fund members?

Difficult $\longleftrightarrow$ Effective

Has the fund ever changed its course in the past?

Never $\longleftrightarrow$ Yes

How do fund members feel about the possibility of changing course now?

Resistant $\longleftrightarrow$ Open

Has the fund ever invited participation from non-family members in the past?

No $\longleftrightarrow$ Yes

How do fund members feel about the possibility of including non-family members now?

Resistant $\longleftrightarrow$ Open to the idea

The history of family wealth creation can often be a challenge to uncover. The stories we hear about the origins of family money rarely form a complete account. These stories often focus on a lone enterprising individual and seldom mention the other people and policies that play a substantial role in financial success.[54] If we want to understand what enables our families' philanthropy to exist, we'll need to look at the full picture.

Here is a list of possible factors to explore when learning more about your family's money story:

- Connections

- Luck

- Inheritance

- Education

- Relationships with banks and investors

- Belonging to a privileged identity group

- Community support

- Family support

- Support from religious and cultural institutions

- Marriage

- Immigration status

- Status in country of origin

- Federal wealth-building programs (like the Homestead Act or the GI Bill)

- Tax breaks, subsidies, and grants

- Labor policies and compensation norms

- Government connections and contracts

- The impact of historical forces that built wealth for some while taking it from others (like slavery or war)

Andy's story

My father died in a plane crash when I was one. I received a large sum of money from the resulting settlement. I want to use that money to bring my family together and effect social change.

I considered creating a family foundation. Between my older sisters, and my mom and me, everyone has different viewpoints. A foundation would make sense as a vehicle for bringing my family closer together. However, we also represent the whole political spectrum, which could hinder the goal of maximum social change. And, the legal structure of a foundation is a work obligation that may not be compatible with the lives and priorities of all my family members. I am now considering other options, such as venture capital or creating a social change organization. In the meantime, I am giving straight out of my investment funds.

I have learned there are a lot of holes in philanthropy. Through talking to people who need funding, I have seen there is a lot of process involved in grantmaking that can really get in the way of their work. The smaller, progressive organizations may not be able to present their work in terms of "projects." This can be a problem for requesting funds from larger foundations.

In my view, activist involvement is of the utmost importance in social change giving. It has to happen if there is to be true change—otherwise there is a power dynamic between the ones with the cash and the ones without the cash that hinders the work. I think that if a funder is truly dedicated to a shift in power, then that funder has to be willing to let go of the decision-making reins at some point. Maybe not fully at first, but it has to happen on some level.

What will success look like? I think success is when existing power structures change—structures that are oppressing people. It's getting to the root of things, stirring things up. To me, it makes sense intuitively that to get the most gain you have got to take risks.

I would still like to use a large portion of these funds to bring my family together. I feel I am mandated to do so, and I believe I can enable this by setting up a scholarship fund honoring my father's love for medical education. I hope that such a fund would provide a level of decision making for the family that serves as a cohesive factor while at the same time freeing me to make high-risk, high-impact social change grants. I would like to give to international social movements as well as funding the organizational capacity of groups working to shift decision making to their constituents. My next step is to search out the things that need the most funding and can create the most change.

CHAPTER 8: IMPROVE COMMUNICATION

Family communication is hard enough *without* trying to run an effective fund. Improving communication is an essential priority no matter what else your action plan entails.

Learn how to recognize family dynamics

In the field of family philanthropy, all the creative ways families communicate and interact with each other has been politely dubbed "family dynamics."[55]

Family dynamics includes phenomena like:

- Sibling rivalries (Lucy took my tricycle.)
- Family hierarchies and adultism (I'm older so what I say goes.)
- Gender dynamics and outright sexism (You could never win at Monopoly because you're a girl.)
- Allegiances (I want Dave on my team.)
- Conflicts (There is no way I am going to be on Dave's team.)
- Power struggles (I made the cookies so I am going to decide who gets to eat them.)

A whole range of family dynamics are also specifically related to wealth. One of the most common is silence. For many families, talking about money is off-limits—which can be particularly inconvenient in philanthropy when money is the main topic.

Unfortunately, family dynamics can get in the way of giving and make it very difficult for non-family members to join in. But once we recognize these dynamics, we can take steps to minimize the impact they have on our philanthropy.

Clarify the decision-making process

If communication melts down whenever your family fund meets, you might need a new decision-making protocol that everyone can understand and respect. Here's an overview of common decision-making methods:

CONSENSUS: Everyone is in agreement. The major advantage of consensus is that all members buy in to the decision. On the flip side, consensus can take a long time and requires commitment from everyone to stick with the conversation.

MAJORITY VOTE: The majority is in agreement. "Majority" can mean over half or another predetermined number (for example, two-thirds of the group). Majority voting can be very efficient and takes much less time than consensus. But it's important to pay attention to the impact of decisions in terms of overall group buy-in. For example, if only 55 percent approve a decision, almost half the members may be unhappy with it.

AUTHORITY: One person makes the final decision—often the chair, president, or founding donor. Authority decision making can be expedient and is great for the person in charge. For everyone else, though, this process can be potentially frustrating.

SUB-GROUP: Decisions are made by a part of the group, often a committee. When a fund is working on developing new policies or plans, this can be an effective way of delegating. Or, if many decisions come up between meetings, an "executive committee" can make operating decisions as needed. It's critical when using this decision-making style that the sub-group keeps everyone else informed.

Plan meetings

One of the best strategies for improving communication is to focus on how meetings are structured. Even the smallest details like lighting and food can change the entire tone. A little planning goes a long way.

THINK ABOUT SCHEDULING

Make sure meeting times are accessible for everyone. Give plenty of notice and send out reminders.

CREATE AN AGENDA

Here are some steps to help you create an agenda:

1) Write down two or three goals. Try not to take on too much at once.

2) Figure out how much time you'll have for the meeting. Block out times for meals, breaks, opening, wrap-up, and informal hang-out time before the meeting begins. Try not to go longer than ninety minutes without a break.

3) Figure out how much time you'll have left to address each goal.

4) For each goal, figure out the best way to structure the conversation. Consider options like guiding questions, case studies, brainstorming exercises, creative projects, and role plays to engage the group. Consider whether the conversation should happen in the full group or might work better in small groups or pairs. Make sure to mix up your formats throughout the agenda because participants will be more or less vocal depending on the size of the group or the activity itself. You may also want to think about strategies for balancing the conversation, like giving everyone the same amount of time to answer a question.

5) Now that you know what needs to happen in the meeting, think about how to set the stage in your opening. Do you need an icebreaker to help everyone warm up? A reflection question to help people get to know each other in a different way? A reading that will inspire the group for the work ahead?

6) Don't forget to explain the ground rules and any other logistics early on.

7) Don't forget to include time for announcements and scheduling.

8) If you're using a "parking lot" (see below), leave time at the end to review.

9) Leave some time in the closing to evaluate how the meeting went. This can be as simple as asking the group "What did you like about this meeting?" and "What would you do differently next time?" Review next steps and make sure everyone is clear about their responsibilities.

10) Think about whether members will need any materials before or during the meeting to accomplish their goals. Distribute everything at least a week ahead of time.

FACILITATION

The facilitator takes responsibility for making the conversation happen and keeps an eye on its flow. If someone is dominating, the facilitator will make sure others have a chance to speak. If the group is getting off topic, the facilitator will reframe the discussion.

It may feel funny to formally structure conversations with family members, but it's a way to ensure that all voices are heard. Consider rotating facilitation from one meeting to the next so that everyone has a turn. Since effective facilitation takes skill, consider attending a training (see the Resource Section).

THINK ABOUT MEETING LOCATION

It's important to find a space where everyone feels comfortable.

Some things to consider:

- Should it be formal or informal?

- Can you find a neutral location not associated with any one person?

- Can you find a space that reflects the values of the fund?

- Is it accessible?

- Is it possible to arrange the seating so everyone can see each other?

- Is there space to break into small groups? Take time out? Go for walks?

- Is there good light?

- Will you have privacy?

SET GROUND RULES

Ground rules govern how all participants behave during a meeting. These agreements help ensure that everyone feels heard and respected in the conversation. Share an initial list with the group at the beginning of the meeting, and then ask for additions or changes. Make sure everyone agrees to the rules before you move on.

Sample ground rules:

- Use "I" statements

- Don't interrupt

- Listen to hear, not to rebuff

- Respect different points of view

RECORD THE CONVERSATION

Recruit someone to take notes so you'll have a common record of the discussion, decisions, action items, and the date of the next meeting. After the meeting, send out a copy of the notes so that everyone has a clear record of what took place.

WATCH THE CLOCK

It's important to respect people's time and not start or end too late. Watching the clock is the facilitator's responsibility. It can also help to have an assigned timekeeper periodically remind everyone how much time is left.

KEEP A PARKING LOT

Often during the course of a meeting issues will come up that could either be the subject of a whole other meeting or should be postponed. Keep a "parking lot"[56] of topics that need to be put off for later, and then come back to them before the meeting ends to decide when and how they will be addressed. This helps everyone stay on track without feeling like their concerns are being dismissed.

FEED PEOPLE

Food can make a big difference—it makes people feel taken care of and helps them focus. It's worth putting thought into the food and drink you're serving and leaving enough time for everyone to eat together.

Open up dialogue between meetings

While the planning of meetings is essential, much of the actual work of improving communication happens *between* meetings. Think about ways to build your relationships one-on-one, like going out for a meal. Invite fund members to attend grantee events or programs relevant to your work together. Make sure there's a consistent method for keeping everyone informed, like a monthly email update or internal website.

Get outside help

Don't forget that outside help is available. Bringing in a professional can be a powerful option, especially in a conflict situation. If it's hard for everyone to hear each other, a facilitator may be able to reframe the conversation. If each family member is on a different page about the fund's mission or goals, a philanthropic advisor can help plan a retreat to find common ground. (See the Resource Section for ideas on referrals.)

CHAPTER 9: RESEARCH SOCIAL CHANGE

If we want to fund social change, we'll need to learn as much as possible about what we're hoping to support. The best way to do this is by listening to the activists out there doing the work.

Get some context

Some places to look for background on an issue or community:

- Local and community-specific newspapers

- Organizational newsletters and websites

- Studies that include information like demographic data, interview material, and policy recommendations

- Activists' essays and biographies

- Art in all its forms, including music, performance, visual arts, poetry, fiction, and film

- Funding dockets (particularly from activist-led funds)

- Idealist.org, a massive database of non-profit organizations around the world

Get involved

Don't underestimate the value of just showing up. Joining in a rally, stuffing envelopes at a mailing party, or listening in at a community meeting are all ways to gain a deeper perspective. Go to talks, actions, festivals, and events. And if you can, volunteer. (Just remember, the idea here is to learn not lead.)

Brainstorm a list of people to talk to

There's no way to avoid it. You're going to have to talk to lots of people. But where to start? Here are some ideas for brainstorming a beginning list:

- What social change organizations are doing this work on a local scale?

- What social change organizations are doing this work on a broader scale?

- Who else could provide more insight on this work? For example: teachers, artists, businesspeople, community group leaders, students, political representatives, journalists, and religious leaders.

- Who else is funding this work?

- Who do I know that could help me meet all these people?

Set up some conversations

When making an initial phone call or email to set up a conversation, here are some important points to include:

- Explain who you are and what the fund is. Give some background on the fund, including its history, grantmaking, and leadership.

- Be clear about the reasons why you'd like to talk.

- Don't give any false impressions about a grant heading their way.

- Share some of the questions you're hoping to discuss.

Be prepared to talk about your role

Especially if you're coming from a family where talking about money isn't the norm, setting up these conversations can be a stressful prospect. Take some time beforehand to figure out how you want to describe your experiences with the fund.

Use these questions as a guide:

- When did you first get involved in the fund? Why?

- What's your role?

- What's your vision of social change?

- How does family philanthropy fit into your vision of social change?

- Where does your family fund currently give? Why?

- What's the current grantmaking process?

- What are your hopes for creating change in your family fund?

- How is this meeting a part of your plan for creating change?

Ask questions

But what will we talk about? Here are some sample questions:

- What inspires you to do this work?

- Will you tell me more about the history?

- What are the main causes of the issues you are working on?

- What strategies do you think have been the most successful? What strategies have been the least successful?

- What are some of the barriers or challenges to doing this work?

- Whom do you collaborate with?

- What is your vision of short-term change? Of long-term change?

- What are the most urgent short-term funding needs? What about ongoing long-term needs?

- What should I read?

- Whom should I talk to?

Reflect

After you've had a number of conversations, don't forget to step back and reflect on what you're learning:

- What are some of the different visions of change that people have shared with you?

- What have you learned about the history and causes of the issue?

- Who are some of the groups doing this work? What have you learned about them?

- How are their missions and strategies similar? How are they different?

- Who is collaborating? How well do you understand the coalitions and alliances between groups?

- Where does funding for this work come from? What have you learned about current funding needs and gaps?

Ashley's story

My great-grandfather started the foundation in the late 1950s. Around the time when my grandmother passed away in the 1990s, there was a huge jump in the foundation's assets. I started attending meetings when I was sixteen.

At the beginning, the grantmaking was piecemeal. My aunt suggested that we get help from the Tides Foundation, and their staff became advisors to the foundation. We had a retreat where we talked for the first time about what the foundation meant to my great-grandfather and my grandparents. As is often the case with family foundations, there was no clear donor intent because the foundation was set up in part for tax purposes. We decided we would fund youth issues.

Working with progressive advisors has had a huge influence on shaping what the foundation is today. We learned how to be grantmakers from them. I remember having early conversations about the irony of being social change philanthropists. Our advisors provided us with an analysis and framework about the different types of organizations we were funding, and how they fit into a bigger picture of youth development and organizing. After a few years of supporting more traditional youth development programs, we discussed the greater impact of organizations that included organizing. We decided to shift our funding in that direction.

We also paid a lot of attention to strategy. I think a lot of family foundations say, "Everybody can do their own thing." But we really wanted to focus on one or two areas. I think about family foundations as having two missions—having a social impact and serving as an instrument for family unity. These two missions can be in conflict a fair amount. Many family foundations do scattershot funding because they want everyone to show up at board meetings, and think they have to let everyone fund separate issues for that to happen. We took the approach that our family should come together around an issue, learn about it, and run an effective business to have some impact.

Recently, we decided that we needed to diversify our assets in a socially responsible way. We have come up with a new set of investment guidelines for the foundation.

In two or three more years we will probably be having conversations about how to go about bringing non-family members onto the board. We've just developed trustee term limits, and we did it in a way that would allow for bringing outside board members in. But this has to be done really thoughtfully. And it's not going to work unless each of us is willing to let go of the power to make grants where we want and to decide what we think is most important. We need to let other people be a part of those conversations. I think that we would probably be a more effective foundation if we became something like the Southern Partners Fund—if we turned over our assets to people who know the field better and are more in tune with community needs. That being said, we would lose the family unity piece, which is really important to me.

CHAPTER 10: SHIFT THE FUNDING

Few families are prepared to make an immediate, dramatic shift in their funding, particularly if they are unfamiliar with the concept of social change. The key to success is grounding your recommendations in the fund's history and current work, and finding ways to make the shift feel like an evolution not a revolution.

Have a preliminary conversation about social change

The first step to making social change an integral part of your fund's work is finding ways to talk about it together. Try to avoid jargon and base explanations on concepts that fund members are familiar with.

- One way to define social change is that it focuses on the root causes of an issue. Propose taking some time during an upcoming meeting for long-term visioning. Ask questions like, "What are the problems the fund is trying to address?" Then brainstorm together about what keeps these problems in place.

- Another way to define social change is that it uses tactics like organizing, lobbying, arts, and popular education to mobilize movement-building. Propose a strategy session. Ask questions like, "What tactics are current grantees using?" Then, share some examples of social change approaches.[57] Brainstorm about how these methods might also be effective.

- Share publications that raise social change issues in ways that resonate with fund members: biographies of inspiring leaders, articles from their favorite journals, and research reports from sources they trust.

Have a preliminary conversation about values

If members have very different ideologies, politics, or perspectives, a dialogue about values can help establish common ground. Here's a sample agenda:

TOPIC: VALUES THAT INFLUENCE OUR GIVING

12:00-12:30   Lunch and hang-out time

12:30-12:40   Review the agenda, meeting goals, and ground rules

Goals:

- Identify the values that are important to each of us and share those with each other.

- Learn how those values influence our philanthropic priorities as a group.

12:40-12:45   Introduce the conversation:

- Each of us comes to family philanthropy with a unique set of values. These values play an important role in guiding our work together.

- This is a useful conversation because it can help us get on the same page and ground our giving.

12:45-12:55   Values cards exercise:

- Give each person a deck of "values cards." You can make these by labeling index cards with one value on each: for example, equity, fairness, respect, peace, empathy, dignity. Include blank cards so participants can add to the deck. (Values cards are also available for purchase.)[58]

- Instructions:

1) You have five minutes to sort the cards. Place the ones that are most important to you on top and the ones that are least important on the bottom. There are blank cards in case anyone wants to add values.

2) Think about a time when you realized how strongly you held one of these values.

12:55-1:20   Group report back:

- Instructions: Share how you sorted the cards, in particular what you chose for your top and bottom cards. You can also share your story of a time when you realized how strongly you held a value. (Allow for three minutes per person.)

1:20-1:50   Group discussion (use flip chart paper to record notes):

- How do our individual values influence our philanthropic priorities?

- How do our collective values shape our family's philanthropy?

- Is our giving in alignment with our values? Why or why not?

- Do we want to make any suggestions for how to move forward?

1:50-2:00   Wrap-up:

- Evaluate the meeting: What did you like about this conversation? What didn't you like about this conversation or what would you do differently next time?

- Next steps: Should we schedule a follow-up conversation?

Make the case

Here are a few strong arguments for shifting funding to social change that other young people in family philanthropy have found successful. Often the trick is translating proposals into the kind of language that speaks best to fund members—even if it doesn't speak to you.

- Use reports and statistics to demonstrate funding gaps and argue for supporting under-funded communities and unmet needs.[59]

- Encourage the fund to take a deeper or more thorough approach. If grantmaking focuses on a specific geographic area, use demographic data to help shift funding toward under-funded and disenfranchised populations. If grantmaking is issue-focused, suggest a wider spectrum of tactics that includes social change approaches.

- If grantmaking priorities are driven by members' individual interests, find ways to connect their concerns to social change. For example, if they are interested in medicine, bring them materials from a community health center. Or, if they are interested in the arts, take them to an exhibit of protest posters.

- If your fund places a high value on innovation, back up your recommendations with materials that frame social change work as cutting edge. Try bringing reports and dockets from other funders that have a reputation for innovation.

- If your fund places a high value on legacy, put your proposals in a historical context and link them back to honoring donor intent.

Propose next steps

If you've generated some interest in social change—even if it's just a spark—there's a good chance that the fund will be able to move toward a deeper commitment over time. Keep in mind that involving everyone in the process of creating a social change funding strategy is long-term work. Here are some potential next steps:

- Suggest a social change grant that fits current guidelines.

- Work with an advisor or consultant to explore current grantmaking priorities and mission through a social change lens.

- Choose two or three potential social change funding areas, and then divide into research committees. Have committees report back to the larger group with proposals for new grantmaking strategies.

- Develop a partnership with an activist-led fund and learn about their grantmaking strategies and dockets.

- Participate in a social change funders' collaborative.[60]

- Allocate a portion of the grantmaking budget specifically for social change. If members aren't ready to make a permanent commitment, suggest a trial period after which they can evaluate the process.

Use discretionary and personal funds

No matter how things are going in your work with your family, you'll always have control over your own giving. If you have access to discretionary funds—or any funds at all—you can still move money to social change.[61] You'll also be building a funding track record that may just inspire your family to follow your lead.

Amy's story

When my dad was brought onto the board no one prepared him. He didn't want that to happen to me, so he actively invited me to foundation meetings beginning when I was fifteen. At first the meetings were kind of intimidating. We'd all have our legal pads out, and I'd use mine to jot down questions to ask my dad afterward.

I also began attending family foundation conferences as a teenager. It was at these conferences that I noticed a major lack of young people. The most striking experience was when, attending a session focused on the next generation, I was the youngest person in the room by at least twenty years.

The foundation was set up by my great-great aunt and uncle. My uncle was a Supreme Court judge in New York State. Technically, the foundation was set up to avoid the estate tax in the 1950s, so about half of his estate went into the foundation before he died. The first board was my grandfather's generation, so I am the third generation of the board but fourth generation of the foundation.

My dad created the adjunct committee to help my generation get involved and as a training program for the board. The committee is made up of family members between the ages of sixteen and twenty-one and the foundation's chairman. Committee members are in charge of making grant decisions with a set of funds, and the chairman is available to give advice.

The foundation is located in and funds the largest but least populated county in New York State. For a long time we were the only foundation in the region. The whole family is from the area so we have a lot of very local connections. I'm trying to think about how to preserve this for the future because I know my generation is already spread out across the country.

Through the foundation it is possible to do so many things to create change. I'd like to find ways to more actively support the gay community in the area. Unless you are in a university, there are no resources available. I'm going to create a survey for high schools to learn about what students want. The foundation has relationships with the guidance counselors at all the high schools, so I can also talk to them. And then instead of us coming in and saying, "This is what you need," we can create something usable for kids who live there.

CHAPTER 11: ASSESS YOUR FUND'S GRANTMAKING

In order to build a case for change in our funds' grantmaking, we need to look more deeply at process. Even funds that don't accept unsolicited proposals or have a formal procedure still follow steps that can be assessed. Keep in mind that answering the questions below won't capture the complexity of the real application process with its time pressures, power dynamics, and sheer volume of writing.

ASSESSMENT: How does the process work?

Accessibility

Is information about the fund readily available? Where? (See sidebar, "Information grantseekers need.")

Is there a publicly listed contact number or email in any of the fund's materials? If so, who responds? How long does it take?

How does the fund determine who is allowed to apply?

Are there any restrictions (e.g., location, size of organization, issue area)? Are these restrictions clear?

Is it clear to grantseekers who makes the funding decisions and how those decisions are made?

Application

How many stages are there to the application process? What are those stages?

What information is requested?

What materials are required?

Are the application materials clear and easy to read?

Is the process accessible to the communities the fund supports (for example, are application materials offered in multiple languages)?

Do any other grantmakers use this application or is it unique to the fund?

How long does the application process take? Are there parts that seem unnecessarily difficult or time consuming?

Follow-up

Does the fund conduct site visits?[62] How are they arranged?

Does the fund commonly request additional materials? How much turn-around time is given?
Does the fund typically schedule follow-up meetings?

Is it clear when the fund will inform applicants about decisions?

What kind of information is given to groups that are denied support? Are they eligible to re-apply? If so, are there additional guidelines or restrictions?

Grantee requirements

Is there a grant agreement letter or some other material that accompanies approved grants?

Are there restrictions on what grant funds can be used for?

What kinds of reports are grantees required to submit?

Are grantees required to attend trainings, meetings, or other events?

Do the requirements asked of grantees seem reasonable?

How else does the fund keep in contact with grantees?

Are grantees eligible to reapply? If so, are there additional guidelines or restrictions?

Are there additional ways the fund supports organizations beyond grantmaking?

Information grantseekers need

In order to make an informed proposal, grantseekers need several types of information:

- Funding guidelines

- Application or proposal form

- Grantcycle and notification schedule

- Overview of the funding process: how decisions are made and who makes them

- Board and staff information

- Past grantees

- Mission statement

- Annual reports

- History of the fund

- IRS Form 990-PF (for foundations)

- Contact information

If the fund does not make this information available, it can be difficult for grantseekers to find it anywhere else. Both Guidestar (www.guidestar.org) and the Foundation Center (www.foundationcenter.org) maintain extensive foundation databases. (Donor-advised funds and charitable trusts are not included.) However these databases are limited to records from tax returns—and do not offer any application information—unless the fund itself provides an update.

How our families feel about giving can dictate the terms of our grantmaking practice. These feelings, though often unspoken, continually influence both the structure of the process and every interaction along the way. An analysis of our families' emotional response to philanthropy will be essential if we hope to make any meaningful changes.

Based on your own observations, how do family members feel about:

- Being involved in the fund?
- Generosity? Gratitude?
- Need?
- Worthiness?
- Trustworthiness?
- Giving? Receiving?
- People who ask for money? Being asked for money?
- People who ask for help? Being asked for help?
- Control?
- Risk?
- Giving anonymously? Giving publicly?
- Being known as a philanthropist?

How do these feelings influence:

- How the fund presents itself?
- How the fund communicates with applicants? Grantees? Partners?
- Funding guidelines?
- Application materials?
- Restrictions on grants?
- Reporting requirements for grantees?
- Relationships with grantees?
- Ideas of success and failure?

David's story

A few years ago, I realized there was no way for me to cleanly separate my activism from the money I inherited and that my family gives. To explore this, I decided to intern at Haymarket People's Fund, an activist-led fund.

During this time, I witnessed many aspects of Haymarket's grantmaking, and became involved in their undoing racism work. As a young, white, straight male of privilege it was a scary experience. Yet I felt supported, and I had the sense that this work was really getting at the root of some of the most basic and entrenched problems in our society. So I had this radical philanthropy experience over the course of about nine months, and I shared bits and pieces of it with my family.

By the end of this internship I had an epiphany: the amount of annual grantmaking at Haymarket roughly equaled that of my family foundation. At Haymarket, dozens of people were involved in raising and distributing money, working together in a very diligent and strategic process. At my family foundation, there was only one person responsible for distributing funds. It was so striking to me that there could be such different ways of making these decisions.

Seeing so many people at Haymarket care so deeply about social change philanthropy inspired me to volunteer for my family foundation. Because the foundation's grantmaking is locally focused and hands-on, I realized the only way I could have an impact was by spending time in the area where it's based. After seeking advice from a number of allies, I became the foundation's first program associate. I stepped into this role without the foundation soliciting résumés from anyone outside the family. It's been uncomfortable to think about this kind of nepotism. At the same time, the position wouldn't exist if I hadn't created it with my parents.

Early on, I went on a site visit for the foundation with my mom. During this meeting, the power dynamics were striking. I noticed that my mother was primarily dealing with the director, and I wondered about how other staff and constituents felt about the work. I had questions that weren't on our "site visit form" for people who weren't in the room. After that, I began to focus on how we run our meetings, how decisions get made, and what forms and applications we use.

Through the trust that has developed between my parents and me, I've been able to introduce the idea of having people outside the family interact with our foundation. Recently we brought in our first outside facilitator to lead a board retreat. We also invited two high school students from a grantee organization to lead us in a training on social change activism.

It's still a really bizarre twilight experience to drive into the town I grew up in and swore I would never go back to in order to go to work. I have had to make an effort to reach out and get advice from peers, to really make connections I wouldn't otherwise have in the office.

CHAPTER 12: TRANSFORM THE GRANTMAKING PROCESS

This chapter looks at how our family funds can open up the lines of communication and create a clearer, more respectful grantmaking process. As you read through the strategies below, keep an eye out for approaches that may resonate with fund members. Do they get excited about efficiency? Focus on streamlining the application. Are they interested in assessment? Start off with a formal evaluation. As always, finding a frame that's familiar to your family can make all the difference.

Conduct a formal evaluation of the fund

An evaluation can provide both a forum for discussion and the necessary information for creating a more responsive process. Methods include surveys, interviews, and focus groups. At a minimum, your evaluation should seek input from past and present grantees. (See Chapter 11 for a starter list of questions.) You may also want to consider including community members, applicants who've been denied funding, partner organizations, board and committee members, and consultants. Using external evaluators and anonymous surveys may help provide more honest feedback.

If members aren't ready to commit to a formal evaluation process, consider sharing reports that document grantee perspectives about philanthropy. (See the Resource Section for examples.)

Make the fund more accessible

Here are just a few ideas for improving communication to make the fund more open and accessible:[63]

- Distribute an annual report or newsletter to inform people about the fund's activities.

- Redesign materials to reflect a commitment to partnership with communities served.

- Set up an extensive website. Make sure it includes all the information a grantseeker needs.

- Update any information that's publicly available about the fund from Guidestar (www.guidestar.org) and the Foundation Center (www.foundationcenter.org).

- Ensure that the contact person is easy to reach and able to respond quickly to grantee and applicant questions.

- Streamline application materials. Don't ask for information you don't actually use. Make sure everything is as clear as possible and easy to read. Avoid jargon.

- Collaborate with other grantmakers to share common applications and streamline the process across funds.

- Translate all materials into the languages used by communities the fund supports. Ensure the fund has the capacity to review proposals and answer questions in these languages.

- Consider where meetings are held. How can the fund go to the communities it serves rather than requiring people to come to the fund?

- Hold an open house so that everybody involved with the fund can meet each other.

Adapt your schedule

Consider how your funding schedule can be more responsive to applicants' needs:

- Learn about the common crunch times in the fields you fund and schedule deadlines for off-times.

- Try to cut down on the time between the proposal deadline and writing the check.

- Offer multiple submission deadlines or a rolling review process throughout the year.

Accept proposals in many forms

Written applications may be one of the most convenient ways to learn about a potential grantee, but they give us a limited view. The ability to work successfully for social change has little to do with the ability to write in the style our families prefer. That's why it's important to give groups the opportunity to present their work off the page.

- Accept videos, photos, outreach materials, publications, and other media as a part of applications.

- Give applicants the opportunity to schedule a time to talk about their proposal and present their work in person or on the phone.

- Ask applicants if there are upcoming events or meetings they would like the fund to attend to see their work in action.

- Go on site visits to get a feel for the organization's space and meet staff and program participants.

Change the way you do site visits

Here are some tips for improving communication during site visits:

- Consult with organizations about scheduling. Be as flexible as possible.

- Prepare questions with fund members ahead of time. Forward your questions to the group before the visit so they know what you're interested in learning.

- If there are specific staff or participants you want to talk to, let the group know beforehand. Be sensitive to situations where meeting with participants may not be possible or appropriate.

- Respect the organization's time. An hour is usually sufficient unless the group requests otherwise.

- Allow time for the staff to ask you questions.

- Be clear with the staff about where you are in your funding process and when you will be back in touch.

- Plan time immediately after the visit for fund members to decide on next steps and follow-up.

- Write a thank-you note to the organization to show your appreciation of their investment of time and energy.

Change the way you evaluate

Funders often have their own intractable notions of success and expect grantee results to fit into that mold. Many also expect grantees to compile extensive reports without considering the amount of time and resources this requires. In order to work toward a partnership model of funding, we'll need to base evaluation more on grantees' visions of success and less on our preconceptions.

- Ask grantees how they evaluate their own success. Consider how the fund could support their capacity to do this.

- Do grantees already create reports for the communities they serve or for other supporters? Could these reports also fulfill the fund's needs?

- Extensive reporting impacts grantees' capacity. If the fund requires this, provide additional support to cover the costs.

Remove funding restrictions

Most organizations, if asked, will explain that what they really need is long-term, unrestricted operating funds.[64] This gives grantees the flexibility to allocate resources based on mission instead of restrictions. Consider revising policies and practices to provide the kind of support grantees need most.

In addition, a great deal of important social change work is currently outside the bounds of what family funds support. Most do not give to international organizations, individuals, or unregistered charities, and avoid funding advocacy activities like lobbying. The laws that guide funds can make these types of grants more complicated and require extra legwork and documentation. However, organizations like the Alliance for Justice and Grantmakers Without Borders can help you to take the necessary steps. (See the Resource Section for references and contact information.)

Offer additional support to grantees

Consider other ways to support organizations beyond giving a one-time gift:

- Provide capacity-building grants

- Provide emergency grants and loans

- Offer mini-grants to attend trainings and conferences

- Share your office space for meetings and events

- Support the organization's fundraising by co-hosting an event

Armando's story

My parents have always been very involved in their community, and they've given their whole lives. In 2001, they came into sudden wealth and decided to start a family foundation. The foundation gives to organizations throughout the Bay Area, mostly in San José, Silicon Valley, and in the Latino community there.

I'm not on the board but I'm involved as a family member. While my parents are interested in changing that, they're not moving quickly which is fine. It frees me up to learn about what it's like to give, how to give, and how to use the power of wealth.

I spend a lot of time thinking about how I can help my parents give. Now that I have a son, I am also motivated to do things that will help the community for the future.

I've been educating my parents about community-based philanthropy—showing them models and introducing them to peers so they're not just hearing it from their son. Recently, my parents wanted to start a scholarship program in one of the school districts in San José. I pointed out that there are different models they could use. They could hand the money over to the superintendent. Or, they could start a committee of people and students from that community to decide where the scholarships should go. I encouraged them not to move too fast and to consider just starting with one school. They really liked the idea of starting slow, and they were open to me helping create a committee.

I am mixing a lot of my work in philanthropy and diversity, trying to involve communities that have not traditionally been a part of philanthropy. I'm starting discussions about diversity within the arts organizations where I work, which tend to be fairly white. I'm also joining development committees at Latino organizations, and partnering with Changemakers to bring a culture-specific donor partner training to the Latino community here. My family is looked to often, because we are people of color, as the ones to ask about diversity. You don't want to be a token, but you can also use it as an opportunity for change if you can be patient.

Recently my parents created a committee for the Latino Film

Festival in San José. They brought community members together to guide the festival. When they told me about the committee I pointed out that they had no young people and no one from the LGBT community. I felt that it wasn't representative. Telling them was a big step.

An important part of family philanthropy is about family dynamics and real honest relationships. As long as the relationships are working, we can work in philanthropy together. When the relationships aren't working, family philanthropy won't work at all. We can have totally different passions and values, as long as we are communicating with each other.

Success in family philanthropy is also about relationships with grantees. We are really close to our grantees because we all live in the same community. For us as grantmakers to have really good dialogue with grantees, we need to not talk so much but open our ears.

CHAPTER 13: OPEN UP THE DECISION-MAKING PROCESS

Family philanthropy must include a broad range of perspectives to effectively fund social change. By calling attention to this, we can make a powerful argument for opening up the decision-making process in our own funds.

Make the case

Here are a few of the most common resistances to opening up the decision-making process and some ways to address them:

"People outside our family won't be interested in participating."

People who are involved in the issues and communities our family is funding have a stake in the direction of these resources. Many other funds have successfully involved non-family decision makers.

"Our meetings are a chance for the family to get together and have meaningful conversations. I don't want to change that."

Involving other people is a chance to have even deeper conversations about the issues our family cares about. As for family time, we can plan a family reunion or vacation.

"Our family is a part of the community we are funding. We don't need anyone else to tell us what we already know."

No one family can represent an entire community's experience. Having access to resources also significantly affects our perspectives. This means that other community members may have a very different understanding of what's going on than we do.[65] If our fund is really going to respond to community needs we have to open up our decision-making process.

"Activists won't be objective. They'll just act in their own self-interest."

Activists are our partners in creating social change. If we believe that they will act in the best interest of their communities as grantees, we need to extend that trust to them in their capacity as fund decision makers. This is an opportunity for them to continue to serve their communities. Furthermore, a conflict-of-interest policy can address how to proceed when organizations that any of us are affiliated with are considered.

Here are a few soundbites that can overcome general resistance:

- "Our grantmaking can be more effective if it's informed by the knowledge and experience of activists and social change leaders."

- "Fresh thinking will help us approach entrenched social problems in new and innovative ways."

- "As funders we have a responsibility to 'uphold the public trust.' The resources we are overseeing are public ones, for public purposes. Shouldn't the public have input in the process of allocating the money?"

- "Shouldn't we be accountable to the communities we fund by including them in the process of deciding where the money goes?"

- "In order to make informed decisions, we should strive to reflect the diversity of the communities we're funding."

Get help making the case
Sometimes the best way to be persuasive is to find someone else to do the persuading. Think about introducing family members to experienced social change philanthropists or academics who can help you make the case. Invite other funders who've opened their decision-making processes to come speak to your family.[66]

Set your course
You'll want to base your course of action on how receptive family members are to the idea of sharing power.

Is your family open to asking for recommendations?

- Invite community and activist advisors to help inform the funding focus through one-on-one meetings or presentations.

- Hold a community meeting with grantees to get feedback on where funding should go in the future.

- Do a series of community focus groups to learn about how the fund could better serve its constituents.

- Consult with social change experts to evaluate your organizational policies.

Is your family open to sharing power?

- Develop a grantmaking committee of community and activist advisors to review proposals.

- Invite grantees to serve on the investment committee and offer guidance about socially responsible investments that could further their work.

Is your family open to transferring power?

- Create a board that includes community members and activists as full voting participants.

- Grant your annual funding budget to an activist-led fund to redistribute.

- Transfer the fund's total assets to an existing or newly formed activist-led fund.

Think about who you're looking for

When funds do invite in non-family members, they rarely seek out people with in-depth social change expertise. Instead, they focus on prestigious degrees and privileged professional associations. While academics, attorneys, and investment advisors may have helpful advice, what's truly missing from family philanthropy is grassroots community leadership. If we're going to help bring these voices to the table we'll need to be intentional about the fund's recruitment process.

First, create a position description that lists the experiences and skills the fund needs. Here are some examples of qualifications you can include:

- Experience in social change activism

- Life experience in the communities funded

- Experience working in diverse groups

- In-depth knowledge of funding focus

- Multilingual

Get the word out

Whether your family fund is opening up a spot on the board or asking for advice, you'll need to be clear about what you're looking for. Think about circulating a formal position description or informal email to help get the word out to activists and community leaders. (See Chapter 9 if you're wondering how to connect to social change networks.)

Important information to include in an announcement:

- Background on the fund, including its history, grantmaking, and leadership

- Reasons for inviting non-family decision makers

- Roles and responsibilities

- Time commitment

- Compensation

- Qualifications for the position

- How to apply for the position

Establish a respectful process

Here are a few things to consider:

- Think about the information you appreciated—or wished you'd had—when you first became involved with your family's fund. What orientation materials or training will new participants need to get the full picture?

- Be sensitive to the amount of time you're asking people to commit in relation to the amount of decision-making power they'll have. Don't ask someone to attend five long meetings just to develop a recommendation for one small grant.

- Respect people's time by covering all expenses and paying them a stipend or honorarium.

- If creating a committee or adding board members, consider using a facilitator to help get the process started.

- Be considerate of people's needs. Help with transportation and childcare. Find an accessible, safe, and comfortable meeting place. Don't forget about food and drinks, and make sure to ask if people have any special needs.

Create a conflict-of-interest policy

Opening up the decision-making process—particularly when including grantees—often raises issues about conflicts of interest. This concern can be effectively addressed by creating a formal policy.

The policy should include:

- Definition of conflict of interest (e.g., involvement in an organization under consideration)

- Disclosure requirement (e.g., to inform all members about the conflict when the proposal is first submitted)

- Protocol for dealing with conflict (e.g., to abstain from voting on grant decisions)

Discuss the fund's long-term commitment

From the outset fund members should consider how non-family participant roles and the commitment to an open decision-making process will evolve over time.

Is this a short-term or long-term position?

- If it's a committee, how long will it last?

- Are there board term limits?

- Will there be opportunities to step into positions of increased responsibility?

- How will people who have cycled out of positions stay connected to the fund?

- How will the fund institutionalize its commitment to an open decision-making process? Will requirements for non-family participation be written into bylaws or other policy documents?

Take responsibility for change

Even when fund members make a commitment to diversity, they often assume that one new participant can represent everyone "like them." Or, they expect a new participant to educate the family on the entire history of oppression. Fund members must instead take responsibility for their own education and respect the individuality of all participants. Inviting just one person will not make a fund automatically more diverse, inclusive, and social change-focused. Nor will it automatically reorient power dynamics.

Family members need to see shifting decision-making power as a complex process that takes time and commitment from everyone. Here are a few ways to get started:

- Use the power assessment in Chapter 14 to compile a report for fund members.

- Anti-oppression trainings can help family members explore assumptions and develop a shared vocabulary. The experience of going through a training together—particularly in situations of conflict—can provide a starting point for dialogue.

- Discuss case studies of how other funds have changed their policies and practices. Consider inviting speakers from those funds to talk about what they've learned.

- Write a diversity statement.[67] Appoint a committee responsible for carrying out the statement concretely.

- Propose a budget item dedicated to ongoing education and reform.

- Hire a diversity consultant to help with facilitation and policy development.

Dana and Tyson's story

Dana: Our mom set up the Phoebus Fund in 1986 because she wanted to include the family in giving. There are four kids, and we were in junior high and high school at the time. She taught us about philanthropy by taking us on site visits and involving us in the grant-making process.

Tyson: I think her idea was to bring more people into philanthropy. She wanted to broaden our understanding about philanthropy's role and potential. For example, on her fiftieth birthday she gave money to ten people she knew in the community—artists, nurses, social workers, teachers, and clergy—so they could choose where the grants should go.

Dana: After she died there wasn't much money in the Phoebus Fund, so we did some fundraising and let it sit for a while to grow. We were able to start giving again in 2001. It is now set up as a donor-advised fund of Bread and Roses, a local grantmaking organization in Philadelphia, and focuses on criminal justice reform. In thinking about our focus area, we asked Bread and Roses, "What areas are not funded? What areas of social change really need our help?"

Tyson: Criminal justice reform is an area that is underfunded but at the nexus of a lot of systems of oppression, from racism to classism. I think we've chosen to focus on this area because it's not an established area of philanthropy like the environmental movement, or even more typical charitable recipients like education or health.

Dana: We have a great partnership with the Bread and Roses Fund. We give them a three-year payout and they do grants research and put out the request for proposals. Bread and Roses has such an extensive network of contacts that we don't have as a family. We need their help to find organizations. In addition, they identified two individuals who serve as community advisors for our grantmaking. One is a professor who teaches criminal justice and the other is an activist who's been really involved in one of the organizations that we fund. Both are now voting members of our grantmaking committee.

Tyson: Philanthropy is such a broad concept. If you're going to give money to your old prep school, I don't think that has very much to do with social change—even if it might be considered philanthropy. I think social change philanthropy requires funding organizations that are not necessarily established, large-budget 501(c)(3) groups.

There's something to be said for having a connection to a fund like Bread and Roses, and local activists that are out there doing day-to-day grassroots organizing. It's really helpful to have a kind of bridge. We are coming from a privileged position and have a very different experience than the inmates and the people who have been oppressed by the prison industrial complex. We have really had to think a lot about issues of diversity in our philanthropy, not just racially, but also in terms of class, gender, and sexuality. It takes more effort to make contact and have conversations with people from small, community-based groups. But the larger organizations typically have the access already, so the social change part requires funders to put themselves out there more.

CHAPTER 14: ASSESS WHO HOLDS POWER

It's hard to include new voices if no one is listening. A seat at the table is meaningless if the real decisions happen somewhere else. Until we look closely at how power operates in our funds and commit to some serious changes, we won't be able to make any change together.[68]

ASSESSMENT

What kind of experience is valued?
What kind of experience do fund members have with social change?

What kind of experience do fund members have with the communities they support?

Is this experience valued in the fund? Is it seen as an important qualification for key decision makers?

Who holds power?
Look at who holds power in the fund in terms of race, class, ethnicity, age, gender, ability, and sexual orientation.

Who's on the board? Who are the officers (e.g., president, secretary, treasurer)?

Who's on committees?

Who's on staff?

Who are the consultants and advisors?

Who makes the grant decisions?

Who has access to discretionary funds?

Who makes the budget decisions?

Who makes the investment decisions?

Who makes the policy decisions?

Who's in a management position?

Who's in a support position?

Do staff have power?

Are staff consulted in major decisions?

Are staff given opportunities for real ownership in the fund—for example, the possibility of making discretionary grants?

What are staff salaries and benefits? Does compensation correspond with the values of the fund?

Who feels at home?

Things like location and office decoration may seem like small details, but they send a strong message about who feels at home in the fund.

Where is the office? Where are meetings held?

What neighborhood is it in? Who feels comfortable in that community?

Are office and meeting spaces accessible to all participants?

What do office and meeting spaces look like? How are they decorated? Whose culture and history are reflected?

What holidays does the fund recognize? How are holidays taken into account when determining proposal deadlines?

When there's food at meetings, what's typically served? Who decides?

What languages are used?

How does the fund celebrate? Who decides what this looks like?

Does the fund have formal policies that address power issues?
Does the fund have a diversity policy? Is it publicly available? Has the fund allocated resources for carrying it out?

Does the fund take diversity into account when making hiring decisions? Recruiting for board and committees? Choosing service providers and suppliers?

Does the fund have an official process in place for making a discrimination complaint?

How does the fund collaborate?
Does the fund collaborate with other grantmakers? Who? How does this get decided?

Does the fund collaborate with identity-based affinity groups and grant-makers?

When the fund invites speakers, who gets considered? How is this decided?

Addressing power and discrimination in our funds is challenging work. This topic is brand new territory for many of our families and can inspire a lot of resistance. Even families concerned with issues of diversity may not realize the depth of commitment required. These questions can help you analyze where family members are starting from, so you can strategize about what's next.

Based on your own observations:

- How do family members understand their class privilege? What are their assumptions about the distribution of wealth? About entitlement? How do they understand the connections between class and philanthropy?

- How do family members talk about race? Is there a shared understanding of racism in general? Of how it operates in philanthropy? How do they understand the relationship between race and class?

- Is sharing power viewed as an ideal or as something threatening?

- Do family members feel it's important to understand the viewpoints of the people affected by their decisions or do they feel they know best?

- How have you seen patterns of prejudice and discrimination play out in your family?

- Are family members willing to talk about these issues? How open are they to change?

- Do family members have any experience with anti-oppression work? Are they willing to stick with a process that may make them feel uncomfortable?

Many of our families look to their cultural heritage to ground and inspire their giving. However, the culture that dominates philanthropy is one that has evolved to help keep power in the hands of wealthy, white people.[69] The norms of this dominant culture permeate everything we do. If we don't find ways to question these norms in the daily functioning of our funds, we won't be able to shift how power is held.

Here are a few examples of these often unchallenged norms:

- There is one "right" answer and only one valid perspective.

- Emotions are disruptive and irrational and should not play a role in decisions.

- Efficiency and measurable outcomes are more important than anything else.

- Information that isn't written down doesn't count.

- Decision makers should feel comfortable at all times.[70]

Based on your own observations, how have you seen these norms affect:

- The way meetings are run?

- The way decisions are made?

- What forms of communication are considered valid?

- Whose opinions are considered valid?

- How feedback and input are incorporated?

- Whether challenges and conflicts are heard or suppressed?

- What is considered effective leadership?

- What is considered an effective non-profit?

Cameron's story

When my family created the foundation about four years ago, my brother and I were involved in helping to choose its area of focus. The foundation funds youth development, civic engagement, and organizing—programs where young people are not just recipients of services but are actually the ones creating change in their own communities.

Because my family started to educate me about my financial resources when I was sixteen, I actually felt pretty prepared to be a part of family philanthropy. They opened up conversations about money early on, so that I wouldn't be told all of a sudden, "Now you have this incredible financial wealth. What are you going to do?"

I've also been able to talk about money with some of my close friends, and I feel really lucky that they're willing to get into it with me. I never want to get so isolated that I'm not challenged about my financial decisions by other people. And to always ask myself questions like, "How do I want this money to factor into my life? How much do I want to give away? How much do I need for myself?" I think instead of putting these questions under the table, I have to bring them to light.

At a recent foundation meeting we had this huge conversation about how much money each board member in my generation of the family should contribute. Some family members would like to see everyone give at a high-level. I'm personally at a place where I would like to give financially, but I'm also very conscious about setting a precedent. I have ten younger cousins who are going to be a part of the foundation in the near future. I don't want to deter them from getting involved by saying, "You have to put in a very large gift to participate." I think we have to make this decision as a group.

It's brought up a number of issues about what it means for us to work together as a family. While everyone in our extended family has inherited wealth, each part of the family takes a different approach to talking with kids about money and their values around money. One of my uncles wanted to wait until after his kids started college to discuss money, as opposed to my parents who wanted us to feel responsible for it at a younger age.

I think we've been able to have some pretty honest and open conversations within the family foundation. If we're not doing some of our own work, how do we expect to build relationships with grantees? We've started to have this whole notion that if we aren't paying attention to our internal work, we aren't going to be fully engaged in the external work. The foundation has actually started to do what my grandparents had really hoped it would do, which is to bring the family together. We are dealing with things that come up because of the different ways we approach the world.

I think success means that we are constantly trying to collaborate, to break off some of the traditional ways of doing philanthropy which is very top-down and where people aren't even addressing the different levels of power at the table. To be really effective we need to constantly evolve and strive to mirror and model the work we see in the programs we fund.

I was talking with someone recently who said that the foundations she knows that are spending down their assets are the ones who've created real urgency. That's something I've been questioning—what will be the length of this foundation? I think we have a real commitment to the fields the foundation is supporting. I also think there's a real desire in the family for the foundation to be passed down. I'm weighing wanting to be personally involved while questioning whether we'll be just another one of those foundations that's set up in perpetuity and doesn't necessarily make a huge impact.

The field of family philanthropy needs a lot of help. There's a certain stagnant way that it's been operating. There needs to be a new infusion of younger voices and conversations about what's next in the evolution of family philanthropy. There are a lot of people who are involved in social change work in their daily lives who have a lot to contribute at the foundation level. They also have the kind of access that could steer foundations in a way that's more responsive to communities they're trying to help, so there's more representation from those communities involved in the decisions.

What will be the footprint of my generation in family philanthropy? I think we need to not be complacent, but to keep asking questions and challenging ourselves to take more risks. It's going to be hard work to not think of this institution as a place where we go home, get together, and make some grants but instead as an ongoing and very intensive involvement in change.

CHAPTER 15: SHIFT THE INVESTMENTS

No matter how much funding we move to social change, most assets remain in investments, not distributed as grants. That's why it's critical we introduce our families to the idea of linking a fund's investments with its mission.

Learn more about the finances
The more at ease we are with the numbers, the more confident we'll be when making the case for Socially Responsible Investing (SRI).

- Use the assessment at the end of this chapter to learn more about the fund's finances.

- Get familiar with reading key documents like budgets, financial statements, and investment reports.

- Take an introductory class on finance and investing.

- Research current writing on SRI. (See the Resource Section for references.)

- Attend a workshop on reading non-profit balance sheets and budgets. (Many philanthropy organizations offer these seminars.)

Have a preliminary conversation
Here's a sample agenda for a meeting about introducing the concept of SRI into the fund's investment strategy. It can be especially persuasive to invite SRI professionals or speakers from funds that have already adopted this approach.

TOPIC: HOW COULD OUR INVESTING FURTHER OUR SOCIAL MISSION?

Pre-reading: Distribute an article ahead of time that provides basic definitions of the concepts.

12:00-12:30   Lunch and hangout time

12:30-12:40   Review the agenda and meeting goals

Goals:

- Learn more about SRI

- Brainstorm options for linking our social mission to our investing strategy

- Determine follow-up

12:40-1:10   Speaker's presentation:

- Overview of SRI

- How SRI relates to philanthropy

- Examples of family funds that have incorporated this approach

1:10-1:35   Brainstorming exercise:

- Hand out copies of the fund's mission, values statement, or grantmaking goals to help everyone focus

- Post flip charts around the room with the following headings:

- It's important that our investments *promote* . . .

- It's important that our investments *avoid* . . .

- Our mission could be advanced by the following business and investment strategies . . .

- Ask everyone to spend ten minutes walking around the room and writing any ideas they have underneath the three questions

1:35-1:55   Debrief:

- Discuss what the group came up with. Ask, "What are your general impressions?" and "What were you most interested in?"

- Ask the group to determine follow-up. More information? Another speaker? Getting technical questions answered? A conversation with grantees?

1:55-2:10   Wrap-up:

- Plan a follow-up conversation

- Discuss the action steps to be taken before that time and who will be responsible for them

Make the case

Here are a few talking points to help address some frequently raised objections to SRI:

"We'll get poor returns."

Incorporating social change goals into investing strategy does not preclude a strong financial return. (See the Resource Section for articles that make this case.) In fact, there are a number of highly profitable SRI vehicles.

"If we focus on returns, we'll have more money to give to the things we care about."

If we change our investment strategy, we can be even more effective by supporting what we care about with 100 percent of our assets.

"SRI is illegal because it risks the foundation's investments."

According to the law, a foundation's assets must be managed "prudently"—in a way that does not jeopardize its ability to carry out tax-exempt purposes. This provision does *not* disqualify foundations from participating in SRI. In fact, many foundations use this investment strategy. (Call the Legal Department at the Council on Foundations if you need an expert to back you up.)

"The companies we've held for the past fifty years have a solid track record. We're not going to change that just because of some new investment fad."

We don't need to sell our stocks to align our investment strategy more closely with the fund's mission. By voting proxies and taking shareholder action we can encourage these companies to become more accountable to social goals.

Propose next steps

Here are some possible next steps you can propose for aligning investments with mission:

- Put the fund's commitment on paper by developing a new investment policy that incorporates social criteria into the guidelines.

- Create an investment committee to oversee this process. Include people with SRI expertise to help evaluate different approaches. Consider inviting grantees to help develop strategies that support their work.

- Meet with a variety of SRI money managers to investigate new investment options.

- Shift a portion of investments into SRI on a trial basis.

- Develop benchmarks that evaluate the social impact of the fund's investments.

- Create guidelines for voting shareholder proxies.

- Join shareholder coalitions to advocate for corporate reform.

- If the fund holds shares in companies where grantees are organizing for change, transfer stock to grantees.

- Make community investments a part of the fund's grantmaking strategy.

- Establish a lending program for grantees and non-profits.

Make your business more socially responsible

Don't forget to consider how the fund spends its resources in day-to-day operations. Take a look at internal policies, such as wages and benefits for staff, to make sure they reflect the fund's values. Examine spending to see how expenses could be bettered align with mission. Some examples: purchase recycled papers, find a minority-owned printing company, order food from a catering company with local produce, host conferences at sites that pay livable wages.

Who manages the assets? How are managers paid?

Is there an investment committee? Who participates?

Is there an investment policy?

Are financial and investment reports distributed and reviewed at meetings? How are these discussed?

Who votes proxies for stocks? Is this person given any guidance on how to vote? Is there a written policy?

Does the investment strategy relate to the fund's mission? If so, how?

Do the board, managers, and staff have expertise in SRI?

Does the fund take its mission into account when making decisions about its day-to-day expenses?

Does the fund have any other types of assets? How do these assets relate to the overall financial strategy?

Chris's story

Learning about my family history on the Rockefeller side has influenced what I feel my responsibilities are when it comes to social change and how I want to move forward. What has been most enlightening is to see how closely connected my family has been to the whole power structure and system that exists today. My family played a role in establishing relationships between government, industry, and banking at the beginning of the last century. These three forces together have created a highly formidable power structure that is intimately linked to the economic and environmental issues we're dealing with today. A lot of what I'm working against is actually largely influenced—and precipitated—by structures and institutions my family helped create.

I'm most involved with the monetary system. My great-grandfather Senator Nelson Aldrich spearheaded the Federal Reserve in 1913. Since it was instituted, this system has placed monetary policy largely in the hands of large banking and industrial interests. We have taken our monetary policy for granted for decades but I believe it's something we must recreate in order to better reflect humanitarian and ecological values. I've been part of a funding circle that makes grants specifically for the development of "complementary currencies"—a way of empowering communities by establishing independent and locally-controlled money.

I have a lot of respect for the many positive accomplishments that my family has achieved through decades of philanthropy. For example, I recently saw that the Rockefeller Foundation had made a grant to Jane Jacobs, one of the radical city planners of the twentieth century.

Yet at the same time, I think it's important to realize how the institutions of philanthropy have evolved alongside our highly unegalitarian economy. Many philanthropic institutions have functioned more as a means of holding onto and expanding wealth and privilege rather than redistributing it. Under the surface, foundations can be a means of influencing public policy and directing private investments. For example, when John D. Rockefeller, Sr. liquidated the Standard Oil Company, both the family and the Rockefeller Foundation—which remained for some time under his influence—maintained shares in all of the companies it was broken into. So my family and all the foundations associated with it continue to hold significant financial holdings and influence in many oil corporations to this day.

Even though several of my families' foundations are becoming more progressive—going closer to the roots of community building and empowering people—I think it's unacceptable that many of the investments are antagonistic to what we're supporting. My family is still heavily invested in one of the world's largest oil companies which is a leading funder of research disputing global warming. If I'm involved in environmental philanthropy, I've got to be concerned about this. There's a tradition that as foundation board members we're not supposed to meddle with the investments. But if you weigh the impact of the investment assets versus the icing that comes off the top for grantmaking, there's just no comparison.

If I became intimately connected to family philanthropy—yet my intent is to create a world in which these structures are unnecessary—how do I reconcile that? I've been intimidated by the immensity of this conflict. But more and more, I think that it's necessary to have some sort of internal influence to transform these institutions from within. My cousin really inspired me when, as a board member of my grandfather's foundation, he succeeded in bringing a campaign to end the Rockefeller Drug Laws onto the foundation agenda and made it a real issue. I was also on the board at the time but had not been so active. It seemed like the whole agenda was set before I got there, yet my cousin's success made me realize that I, too, could have an impact.

Though I have had minimal experience in my family's philanthropy, I would like to bring some of these concerns to the table. I think the individuals within the institution need to become more self-reflective. What are these structures really about? I think it's been more about maintaining power and privilege than dealing with the underlying problems of society. That's what I think needs to come out and be acknowledged. These institutions have protected certain wealthy families, but the cost has been many of the disastrous things happening in the world. There needs to be a dialogue in family foundations that really brings up these fundamental questions. What I'm up against is decades and decades of family members walking in line to a structure in which the primary rule is to not touch the principal.

CHAPTER 16: DEVELOP A PAYOUT PLAN

Perpetuity is one of the most difficult topics to broach in family philanthropy. Talking about how long our funds will exist brings up intense feelings about money, relationships, and power. It forces people to think about transition and loss. Moreover, it requires questioning our families' right to steward these resources in the first place. Challenging perpetuity is also one of the most dramatic ways we can commit our funds to social change.

Take preliminary steps

Here are a few approaches to consider:

- Use the assessment at the end of this chapter to examine your fund's current thinking on perpetuity and determine where you're starting from.

- Interview other family funds about their payout plans. Invite them to speak at a meeting or present a summary of your findings.

- Seek out grantee perspectives about the fund's future and duration. Working with an independent interviewer may help you get more open feedback.

- Hire a facilitator to help guide a preliminary conversation on perpetuity with all fund members. Focus on exploring options for aligning the fund's future plans with mission.

Make the case

Here are a few potential talking points you can use to help fund members take a fresh look at perpetuity:

- "Redistributing the bulk of our assets instead of just a small percentage would more effectively further our philanthropic mission."

- "While an aggressive payout strategy may mean fewer philanthropic opportunities for the next generation, we will benefit even more from the change that increased giving helps create."

- "The fund has always placed a high value on passing the torch to the next generation. That's why, as the next generation, we want to step more fully into our responsibilities and help not only with grantmaking but also with long-term planning."

- "Family legacy has been an essential part of our philanthropy over the years. However, there are many ways we can honor this legacy that don't require holding onto these funds in perpetuity."

- "Grantees can benefit from the stability that comes with a permanently endowed fund. Yet we still need to question our family's permanent role in distributing the fund's endowment."

Start developing a plan

If you've been able to build some interest in questions of perpetuity and payout, fund members may be ready to take the next step and start drafting an actual plan. This plan can be your roadmap for distributing a large portion or even the entirety of the fund's assets by spending down or transferring them. Creating a payout plan is a long-term project, so don't get frustrated because it *will* go slowly. You may want to consider getting some outside help from a consultant.

Payout plan goals may include:
- Increasing or expanding grantmaking

- Endowing grantees

- Transferring the fund's assets to an activist-led fund

- Transferring control of the fund to an activist board

Here are some questions the plan will need to address:
- How long will the fund exist?

- If spending down, what portion of the assets will be distributed? How will this be carried out?

- If transferring assets to an activist-led fund, how will this partnership be developed? What will the process look like?

- If transferring control to an activist board, how will new members be identified? What will the process look like? Who will help facilitate the transfer of power?

- How will grantees participate in the process?

- How will staff participate?

- After a transfer, will family have a role? What will it be?

- Who will be responsible for carrying out this process?

- What's the projected timeline?

- How are these payout goals in line with the fund's mission?

ASSESSMENT

Do the bylaws or trust documents mandate a certain duration for the fund? Or bind the fund to donor intent? Can these be altered? By whom?

Does the family rely on the fund to fulfill estate-planning goals (e.g., for tax deductions or for passing on an inheritance through a charitable trust)?

Does the family rely on the fund to foster unity (e.g., to bring together dispersed family members)?

Does the family rely on the fund to pass on values to the next generation (e.g., to teach children about giving)?

Does the family rely on the fund to fulfill legacy goals (e.g., to build social standing or to commemorate family members through named gifts)?

What is the current level of family involvement in the fund? Are there plans for building future family involvement?

How do family members feel about their participation in the fund? Is it viewed as a valuable opportunity or a burden?

Is the fund currently in transition or are there major transitions on the horizon (e.g., a shift in assets, the passing of a family member, or turnover in board or staff)?

Leslie and Heeten's story

The Global Environmental Health and Justice Fund is a donor educa-tion circle housed at The New World Foundation (NWF). Many partic-ipants in the circle are members of family funds. Leslie—a family foun-dation trustee—and Heeten—a program officer at NWF—describe how the fund developed.

Leslie: I'm a trustee of two different family foundations. I contacted Heeten, the program officer for environmental justice at NWF after taking a workshop at Resource Generation on creating a giving plan. I had decided that a third of my giving would go to environ-mental justice and I needed to learn more about it.

Heeten: I was hired in 2000 as a program officer at NWF after being a grantee for several years. In the months before Leslie contacted me, I had been talking with the staff about how we could leverage more resources to fund global environmental issues. Leslie and I talked about the idea of a pooled fund where we both brought dif-ferent resources to the table. We left our first meeting with the idea that Leslie would reach out to other young donors, and I would bring NWF's experience with funding to create the Global Environmental Health and Justice Fund (GEHJF).

Leslie: A trust started to build between Heeten and me after our first meeting. We talked for several months about how the GEHJF would work. It was set up so the NWF board would decide where grants go, and donors would participate in programs to learn about the funding. I was really grateful to be connected to an organization that had the experience of doing strategic funding. It felt like the decision making was "clean"—it wasn't people from the outside coming in and making decisions about how funding should happen. It was a really different dynamic, one that could potentially be more effective in the long term. As donors of the GEHJF, we had to be mindful of the fact that we were working with an institution that had its own structure.

Heeten: At NWF, program staff solicit proposals from the field, go on site visits, and present a docket to the board. Our board is made up of practitioners, current and former grantees, and movement thinkers. They are the ones that make the final decisions.

By establishing the GEHJF so that donors would learn about the issues but not make grant decisions, we were experimenting with something new. The fund was going to grow because it would attract people who liked the structure. We now have fourteen donors that participate in the circle, and each person gives or raises a minimum of $5,000.

Leslie: Donor education has become a part of what the circle is about. Donors meet twice a year to review the docket and learn about the issues we're funding. For example, at one meeting we focused on groups in India and read articles about how their growing economy impacts pollution. We've also had guest speakers from grantee organizations. A few people have brought their family members to the meetings.

Being involved in the GEHJF has affected my own engagement with family philanthropy in a number of ways. I've given to environmental justice, and I ask different questions of the groups I am funding—questions about how the organizations are thinking about leadership development, and how conscious they are about race in their work. I've also been able to encourage a few organizations to apply to my family foundation for multi-year grants. While the donor circle has felt like something I can do separate from my family, I've also been thinking about how I can make suggestions for my family's giving—to step forward and put aside some of the baggage about what I think they will be open to.

CHAPTER 17: SHARE YOUR PHILANTHROPIC POWER

The fact is, family philanthropy grants us a lot of power. We have access to influential connections. We can publish reports and publicize causes. Our family funds can legitimize—and even define—what issues are important. And the more involved we become, the more power we get.

While much of this philanthropic power isn't transferable, we can still strive to share it with activists and grantees. We can use our institutional access to help transform the institution itself. Our success will rely on building strong, respectful partnerships.

Share your access

One way we can share philanthropic power is by collaborating with activist partners on programs and publicity. Our access and clout can help open doors and get their message out.

- Collaborate on a report or press release.

- Develop conference sessions, panels, and workshops together. While many philanthropy conferences are funder-only, activists can attend if they are speakers.

- Write articles and op-eds for philanthropy media and journals.

- Co-sponsor an event or program.

Share your connections

Having a family fund—and the class privilege that comes with that—means we've got some powerful connections. We can leverage these connections to influential decision makers by sharing our contacts.

BRAINSTORM CONTACTS

The first step is to brainstorm a list of everyone you can rope in. Think about:

- Funders, including board and committee members and staff

- People from philanthropic membership organizations or conferences

- Philanthropic advisors

- Fundraisers

- Financial advisors and investment managers

- Lawyers, especially those who specialize in estate planning

- Government and elected officials

- Business leaders

- Journalists, editors, writers, and producers

- Professors and deans

- Fellow students and alumni

- Family members

- Neighbors

- Co-workers

- Family friends

- Fellow members of cultural, religious, or civic groups

- Fellow volunteers

PUT THOSE CONTACTS TO USE

Here are some ways to do this:

- Invite people to attend social change events and programs.

- Help place an article about a group's work in the media.

- Bring a key decision maker to the table for a meeting or negotiation.

- Enlist the support of a local leader for a campaign.

- Set up meetings to connect activists with potential supporters.

Make sure to share these contacts in a respectful way. Be considerate of people's preferences for privacy and anonymity, and always ask permission before passing on any information.

Be a part of the big picture

What does it take to get social justice movements the resources they need? A number of groups are asking this question and coming up with strategies for big picture change.

Organizations like the National Network of Grantmakers and the National Committee for Responsive Philanthropy are seeking to transform foundation policies, practices, and power dynamics on a fundamental level. They are educating funders about how to use decision-making structures that are more open and diverse. They are also broadening the definition of institutional philanthropy so that it's more inclusive of giving across culture, race, gender, age, sexual orientation, ability, and class.

Groups like Grassroots Institute for Fundraising Training, Grassroots Fundraising Journal, and INCITE! Women of Color Against Violence are looking at how the practices of institutional philanthropy impact the direction of social justice movements. They have found that the enormous control wealthy donors hold often undermines activists' goals. These groups are working to create alternative funding methods to transfer donor-power to the grassroots.

It's crucial that we connect the work we're doing in our family funds to the larger picture by joining coalitions, participating in conferences and events, and lending our support. Check out the Resource Section for many of these groups' contact information.

Speak out about funder-only restrictions

Many of the organizations that shape philanthropy and set its policy are often restricted to funders only. This blocks grantees from having a voice in defining the field. Here are some ways we can use our philanthropic power to advocate for change:

- Strategize with activist partners and grantees about how to raise this issue with other funders.

- Whenever you're in a restricted-access space, call attention to it. Remind participants that important perspectives and experiences are missing.

- Seek out opportunities to influence policy by joining governing committees and boards or, if possible, nominating activists for these positions.

Share your work

Don't underestimate the influence that comes with philanthropic access. You can have an impact just by talking about your work and your commitment to social change philanthropy with other funders. Attend conferences ready to network. Keep copies of articles and backup materials with you at all times. Get in touch with advisors and suggest publications they can pass on to other funders. And last but not least, seek out young people involved in family funds and offer support.

Sharing power is complicated. Even with the clearest intentions, the reality can be murky. What does it mean that we still get to decide with whom we share our power—or even *if* we share it at all? How can we stay conscious of the power we're using and not lose sight of why we have it in the first place? There may not be any easy answers to these questions, but we'll need to constantly challenge ourselves to ask.

- How do we decide with whom we share our access and connections?

- Where is the line between building our access and connections so that we can use them for social change and building them for our own benefit? What about if we're building them for social change and benefiting at the same time?

- What's the difference between using our philanthropic power to leverage funding for something we are directly involved in versus something we are not directly involved in?

- What's the difference between inviting activists into funder-only spaces and speaking on their behalf?

- How can we help activists build their own relationships with funders instead of requiring activists to continually pursue these connections through us?

- Where is the line between working within the system to change it and just becoming a part of it?

- Are there people in our lives who challenge us on these questions? If not, why?

CHAPTER 18: CREATE AN ACTION PLAN

An action plan can help you move from ideas to implementation. It's a useful format for prioritizing goals and creating a workable timeline. On the following pages you'll find an action plan template and some guiding questions.

Visioning

Write your vision statement for creating change through family philanthropy. Don't worry if it's polished—the important thing is to record some of your core ideas. This vision will shape your goals and help you keep an eye on the big picture.

- What are some of the beliefs that inspire you to do this work?

- What role do you hope your family fund will play in social change?

Goals

Goals help you turn a big vision into specific intentions. Come up with three things you hope to accomplish by the end of the year that will bring you closer to your vision.

- These goals could include:

- Issues you want to raise

- Proposals you'd like to create

- Relationships you want to build

- What you hope to learn

Action steps

While goals state what you intend to accomplish, action steps are what you'll need to do to achieve them. Brainstorm a list of possible actions for each goal.

- What information do you need?

- Who do you know that could help?

- Whom do you need to talk to? What would be the most effective way to frame the conversation?

- If this requires educating fund members, what techniques do you think would be helpful?

- If this is a proposal, what steps do you need to take before making it? What's the protocol for doing so? What would be the most successful way to present it?

Support team

A support team can help you stay on track. Set periodic dates to check in about how your plan is going.

Think about including people who:

- Are also doing this work with their family.

- Have activist experience in the field you are funding or in social change in general.

- Work with an activist-led fund.

Evaluation

Set dates to reflect on your progress. Spend some time thinking about the following questions and talk the answers over with your support team.

- What are some of the steps I have taken?

- What am I proud of accomplishing?

- What is going well?

- What has been challenging?

- What has been surprising?

- Am I avoiding anything in my plan, and if so, why?

- What do I want to do differently as I move forward?

- Are my goals realistic? Why or why not?

- Am I asking my support team for help when I need it? Do I feel like I'm getting the support I need to stick to the plan?

- What else do I need to be successful?

ACTION PLAN

This plan is for the following year(s): _____

My vision for creating change through family philanthropy:

_____

_____

_____

Goals

1. _____

2. _____

3. _____

Action steps	Timeline
For goal #1:	
For goal #2:	
For goal #3:	

Support team members:

_____

_____

_____

When I'm feeling discouraged, I should remember this because it always inspires me:

_____

_____

I'm going to evaluate and adjust my plan every _____ months.

Notes:

_____

_____

_____

_____

_____

_____

_____

_____

_____

_____

_____

_____

Tips for sticking to your action plan

- Start now. You don't need to know every single detail about your family fund to begin the process.

- Pace yourself. Don't try to do everything at once.

- When choosing deadlines, pad your time estimates. This work can take awhile.

- Devote a specific time in your weekly calendar to your plan.

- Don't underestimate the emotional drain that can come with this work. Make sure to give yourself time to reflect and recharge.

- Don't get bogged down by the past. As history has shown, change is possible even when it seems like the odds are against it!

CONCLUSION

Almost every chapter of this book has stated how hard, incremental, and slow creating change through family philanthropy can be. It can take years before fund members see eye-to-eye on what change means, much less take action. Moreover, the institution of family philanthropy controls hundreds of billions of dollars—many people have a vested interest in keeping things the way they are.

But there is so much at stake. We are about to see the largest intergenerational transfer of wealth in history. It's estimated that at least $41 trillion will change hands in the next fifty years.[71] And we are part of the very small group of people who will have a say in where that money goes. After all, 70 percent of the wealth in the United States is controlled by only 10 percent of the population.[72]

Imagine the possibilities if we could redirect some of these resources toward social change. Imagine if we could open up family philanthropy's decision-making table to more than just the wealthy few. We have inherited the power to make a change. With persistence and dedication, we can ensure that the *next* "next generation" will inherit something very different from the philanthropy we know today.

APPENDIX

You probably won't hear anyone talking about the institution of philanthropy. But, you will hear people refer to "the field." The philanthropy field encompasses funds of all types (including those that are family- and activist-led). It also includes a variety of <u>infrastructure groups</u>[73]—organizations that are set up to promote giving.

Types of funds

The philanthropic field includes a wide range of funds. For example, <u>community foundations</u> are public funds that support a geographic area. <u>Giving circles</u> are pooled funds in which members make grants together.

Infrastructure groups

Infrastructure groups come in many forms. <u>Membership organizations</u> and <u>research organizations</u> provide conferences and publications on grantmaking and governance. Some also lobby on philanthropic policy. These include (here come the acronyms):

- Association for Small Foundations (ASF)

- Council on Foundations (COF)

- Independent Sector

- National Center for Family Philanthropy (NCFP)

- National Committee for Responsive Philanthropy (NCRP)

- National Network of Grantmakers (NNG)

- The Foundation Center

- Regional Associations of Grantmakers (RAGs)

<u>Affinity groups</u> connect funders that share a common interest or identity. Asian American/Pacific Islanders in Philanthropy (AAPIP) and Grantmakers Without Borders (GWOB) are two examples.

<u>Philanthropic advisors</u> are consulting firms and individual consultants that assist funds with everything from accounting to grants research to meeting facilitation.

A growing number of universities have established <u>research centers</u> and <u>degree programs</u> focused on philanthropy and the non-profit sector. The Center on Philanthropy at Indiana University and the Center for Social Innovation at Stanford University are just a few examples.

A non-profit organization (or "non-governmental organization") is a group with a social mission. Rather than create profits for owners or investors, non-profits use all of their income to advance social goals.

Most non-profits are set up as public charities, sometimes called "501(c)(3)s" (referring to the part of the tax code that defines them). Public charities must demonstrate to the IRS that they receive broad public support. Public charities can offer tax deductions to their contributors and are eligible for tax exemption themselves. This type of non-profit faces limitations on lobbying.

Social welfare organizations, or "501(c)(4)s," have a greater ability than public charities to participate in lobbying, political campaigns, and legislative advocacy. However, contributions to these groups are not tax-deductible for supporters.

Professional and trade associations, or "501(c)(6)s," include organizations that promote the business or professional interests of a community or industry.[74]

Family foundations give grants to non-profit organizations, generally to those that are public charities. Confusingly, some foundations are *also* incorporated as non-profits. But they still follow the same basic rules as other private foundations (see "The Foundation Rulebook").

FAMILY FOUNDATIONS

A <u>foundation</u> is an organization that gives away or uses money for charitable purposes. According to the Council on Foundations, a family foundation is "one in which the donor or the donor's relatives play a significant governing role."[75]

The vast majority of family foundations are set up as <u>private foundations</u>. These funds typically receive money from one source and are required to give away an average minimum of 5 percent of their assets each year. (See "The Foundation Rulebook" for more details.) Some are incorporated as non-profits while others are established as trusts, though this difference doesn't have a significant impact on how foundations are run. <u>Operating foundations</u> are private foundations that can also run their own programs.

Here's a summary of "the rules"—the minimum legal requirements for family funds set up as private foundations. While it doesn't cover the minutiae of the law, this overview can give you a sense of the fundamentals.[76]

Rule #1: Create a system of governance

Most foundations are set up as non-profit corporations and therefore governed by a <u>board of directors</u>. Foundations established as trusts have a <u>board of trustees</u>. However, these two terms—and the functions associated with them—are often used interchangeably.

Board members have <u>fiduciary responsibility</u> to the foundation, including the "duty of care," "duty of loyalty," and "duty of obedience." Together these terms describe board members' obligations: attending meetings, making informed decisions, and ensuring that the fund meets legal requirements and acts according to mission.[77]

In some states there is a minimum age requirement or number of participants for boards. Foundations often create policies outlining who is eligible to serve—for example, relatives by blood or marriage of the original donor—that go beyond these statutes.

Foundations set up as non-profits have <u>articles of incorporation</u> which include <u>bylaws.</u> This document describes the governance process and names the <u>officers</u> of the fund (e.g., chair, treasurer, secretary). Foundations established as trusts document their guidelines in the form of a <u>trust agreement</u>.

Rule #2: Establish why the foundation exists

Foundations must be "organized and operated exclusively for religious, charitable, scientific, testing for public safety, literary or educational purposes . . ." Each new foundation files a statement of its <u>charitable or tax-exempt purposes</u> with the IRS. In addition, many boards adopt a <u>mission statement</u> to describe their grantmaking intentions.

Rule #3: Give money each year for charitable purposes

A foundation must distribute at least 5 percent of its average annual assets to further its charitable purposes. This is called <u>payout</u>. <u>Qualifying distributions</u>—the funds that count toward payout—include grants and reasonable administrative expenses. A foundation also pays a yearly <u>excise tax,</u> comprising 1 or 2 percent of net investment income, depending on the size of its payout.

Foundations can make grants to almost any type of organization or to individuals, as long as the purpose of the grant is "charitable" under federal law. However, most family foundations give exclusively to public charities based in the United States. In order to give to other types of groups, a foundation needs to ensure that the funds will be used for charitable purposes and not for politics or private gain. <u>Expenditure responsibility</u> is the documentation the IRS requires in these circumstances.

Rule #4: Invest the assets responsibly

The assets must be managed "prudently"—in a way that does not jeopardize the fund's ability to carry out its tax-exempt purposes. In addition, a foundation and its "disqualified persons" (see Rule #5) cannot own more than 20 percent of the voting stock of a business.[78]

Rule #5: Don't manage, give, or spend money in a way that benefits the people involved.

<u>Self dealing</u> involves a transaction between the foundation and a <u>disqualified person</u>, such as the sale of property, lending of money, or use of income or assets for personal benefit.

Disqualified persons include:

- Trustees, directors, managers, or officers of the foundation.

- Substantial contributors to the foundation.

- An owner of more than 20 percent of any business that is a substantial contributor.

- Family members of any of the above, including spouses, children, grandchildren, great-grandchildren, parents, other ancestors, or spouses of children, grandchildren or great-grandchildren.

- Any corporation in which more than 35 percent of the voting power is owned by disqualified persons.

- Certain government officials.[79]

These rules don't bar board or family members from reasonable compensation for professional services provided to a foundation.[80]

Rule #6: Report to the government and the public

Many of the laws governing foundations are federal, and the Internal Revenue Service (IRS) is charged with ensuring that foundations run responsibly. States also monitor operations since a foundation is bound by the laws of the state where it is based.

In order to be recognized as tax-exempt, foundations must file an <u>IRS Form 1023</u>. They must provide a copy of the governing documents, a statement of projected activities, information about trustees, a balance sheet, and a budget. Each year, foundations also submit an <u>IRS Form 990-PF</u>, providing information about assets, investment income, donations, salaries, expenses, and grants.

Foundations are required to provide copies of the three most recent Forms 990-PF to anyone who requests. In addition, foundations that are organized as non-profit corporations must make their <u>minutes</u>—a record of business at board meetings—available to the public. Many funds choose to create an <u>annual report</u>—a yearly summary of their activities—to distribute broadly.

There is no universal way that family foundations make grants. However, this template provides a sketch of some common steps.

While board members typically reserve the authority to make final allocation decisions, they may hire staff or advisors to assist with grant-making. Program officers, program associates, or philanthropic advisors may oversee the process. Boards also sometimes convene grantmaking committees to do this work.

The complete process is often referred to as a <u>grant cycle</u>. The grant cycle may take place once a year, several times a year, or it may stretch out over a few years.

In the first part of the process the foundation identifies its <u>funding priorities</u>—the issues and/or communities it will give money to. These priorities may be shaped by the board, staff, or a grantmaking committee. Some family foundations never go through this stage, giving to a wide range of issues and/or communities. This process is sometimes referred to as <u>checkbook-style grantmaking</u>.

The next part of the grant cycle involves organizations asking the foundation for money. Some foundations publish <u>grantmaking guidelines</u> or <u>requests for proposals</u>. These documents describe who should apply and how to go about it. Sometimes, this stage becomes a two-step process: applicants first submit a <u>letter of inquiry</u>—a shorter version of their proposal. The foundation then decides whether or not to invite a full proposal.

After the <u>proposal deadline</u> has passed, the foundation reviews the requests that have been received. Staff or advisors may be responsible for writing up summaries and recommendations. They may also arrange <u>site visits</u> to see organizations' operations and meet staff. The foundation then decides which groups will be awarded grants. This decision typically rests with the board.

The foundation then awards grants. Organizations that will not be funded may receive a <u>declination letter</u>. Organizations that will be funded may receive a <u>grant agreement letter</u>. Besides informing an applicant that their proposal was successful, this letter articulates the size of the grant, what it's intended for, and any terms, restrictions, or reports required. Organizations that are not funded are rarely informed of the reasons why.

The final stage of the grant cycle is reporting. Foundations often require <u>grant reports</u>—a summary of what an organization accomplished with a grant. Some funders ask for reports after a year, while others prefer to track progress as often as quarterly. Some foundations hire external evaluators to provide ongoing monitoring of grantees.

Many family foundations don't actually publicize their funding criteria or consider unsolicited proposals. They simply give money to organizations they already know, often by requesting proposals from select groups. This is called a <u>closed process.</u>[81] In these cases, it's impossible for organizations not already known to a funder to request money.

DONOR-ADVISED FUNDS

A donor advised fund is set up as a distinct account within an existing public foundation.[82] The <u>advisor</u>—often the original donor, along with their family—offers advice about where grants should go. Some funds also allow the appointment of a <u>successor advisor</u>—the person charged with giving advice in the future. That person is frequently a member of the next generation.

A wide range of foundations have donor-advised fund programs—from social change-oriented funds to those associated with private banks. Up until now, each program has had its own set of rules. Policies for how much money must be distributed, where grants can go, and how long a fund can exist have been left largely to a foundation's discretion. The Pension Protection Act of 2006 recently established new provisions for how donor-advised funds can be used. While there will continue to be some variation among programs, this act sets new parameters on practice. For example, donor-advised funds must now follow disqualified persons rules similar to those for private foundations, and exercise expenditure responsibility for certain types of grants. (See "The Foundation Rulebook" for an explanation of these terms.) At the time of this writing, the nuances of this new law are still being discussed.[83]

Donor-advised fund grantmaking takes many forms, though few funds accept unsolicited proposals. Some use an extensive grant cycle—including proposal forms, site visits, and grant reports—while others are much more informal. In many cases the staff of the foundation where a fund is housed provides advice and support.

One of the most significant differences between donor-advised funds and family foundations is the authority fund members have. In foundations, decision-making power rests with the board. In donor-advised funds, family may *advise* the host foundation about where to direct money, but don't have the final say. However, the host foundation rarely goes against the family's recommendations.

CHARITABLE TRUSTS

A <u>trust</u> is a legal device for setting aside money or property for the benefit of people or organizations. Charitable trusts allow money to grow and get transferred to both individuals and non-profits while reducing estate, income, and gift taxes. Although a private foundation may take the form of a trust, the term "charitable trust" usually refers to charitable remainder and charitable lead trusts. These entities were created in the Tax Reform Act of 1969.

A charitable <u>remainder trust</u> provides annual income to a non-charitable beneficiary—typically the donor, their spouse, or other family member—for a designated period of time. The trust then transfers all remaining property to designated non-profits or a family fund. A <u>charitable lead trust</u> starts out by making annual distributions to non-profits, and then gives its remaining assets to the non-charitable beneficiary—whether a family member or someone else.

A charitable trust can support non-profit organizations that meet the charitable purposes described in its <u>trust document</u> (the legal paperwork used to set it up). The donor and trustees have the power to decide where the money goes. A charitable trust's lifespan is often long—decades or even generations—so the principal has time to grow while paying few or no taxes.

Charitable trusts must file forms with the IRS: Forms 1041, 1041-A and 5227 for charitable lead trusts, 1041-A and 5227 for charitable remainder trusts.

Here are some of the main roles young people play in their own family funds:

- Serving as members of a foundation board: As foundation board members, young people are responsible for governance, grantmaking, and other duties.

- Joining a junior or next generation board or adjunct committee: Some funds set up next generation boards to involve and educate young family members about philanthropy. Members are typically given an allowance of grantmaking money to allocate as a group, though foundation boards typically reserve power of final approval.

- Building a next generation fund: A new, autonomous fund is created for the next generation to run. Its assets may come from the contributions of family members or an older fund.

- Allocating discretionary funds or matching grants: A next generation member may allocate discretionary funds[84] to issues they are personally connected to, though often pending final approval from the larger group. Matching grants are available to increase a personal gift of time or money by a young person to a qualified organization.

- Participating in educational opportunities: This may take many forms, such as: finding a mentor, networking with peers, going on site visits, interning, serving on foundation committees, facilitating meetings, creating a giving plan, participating in a giving circle, volunteering for a non-profit, and attending conferences and workshops.

- Serving as fund staff: Young people work as volunteer or salaried members of their family fund's staff.

- Making decisions for a donor-advised fund: While donor-advised funds typically designate one person as an official advisor, that person may involve young people in decisions about where funding should go.

- Becoming successor advisors for a donor-advised fund: A member of the next generation is appointed as the fund's primary advisor when the original advisor is no longer involved.

RESOURCES

Below are a variety of resources that can help you follow-up on the topics discussed throughout the book. Of course there are many, many more articles, books, and organizations, but hopefully this will provide some places to begin. Descriptions of organizations are included only when it's not apparent from their names what they do.

Resource Generation
www.resourcegeneration.org

Karen Pittelman and Resource Generation. *Classified: How To Stop Hiding Your Privilege and Use It For Social Change*. New York: Soft Skull Press, 2006.

Courtney Young. *Privilege and Protest: Young People With Wealth Talk about Class and Activism*. Cambridge, MA: Resource Generation, 2003.

Courtney Young. *Voices Carry: Young People With Wealth Talk about Silence, Guilt and Social Change*. Cambridge, MA: Resource Generation, 2003.

History of institutional philanthropy
A starter list . . . For a more extensive one, see the philanthropy bibliography from the Swearer Center for Public Service at Brown University (www.brown.edu/Departments/Swearer_Center/scholarship/ycfbiblio.shtml).

Robert Bremner. *American Philanthropy*. Chicago: University of Chicago Press, 1960.

Peter Dobkin Hall. *Inventing the Nonprofit Sector and Other Essays on Philanthropy, Voluntarism, and Nonprofit Organizations*. Baltimore: Johns Hopkins University Press, 1992.

Waldemar Nielsen. *Inside American Philanthropy: The Dramas of Donorship*. Norman, OK: University of Oklahoma Press, 1996.

Thomas A. Troyer. *1969 Private Foundation Law: Historical Perspective on its Origins and Underpinnings*. Washington DC: Council on Foundations, 2000.

A sampling of perspectives on philanthropy
Critiques of philanthropy come from all different angles. Here's a mix of perspectives:

Andrew Carnegie. "Wealth." *North American Review* CXLVIII (June 1889): 653-64.

Charles T. Clotfelter and Thomas Ehrlich, eds. *Philanthropy and the Nonprofit Sector in a Changing America*. Bloomington: Indiana University Press, 1999

Mary Ann Culleton Collwell. *Private Foundations and Public Policy: The Political Role of Philanthropy*. New York: Garland Publishing, 1993.

Mark Dowie. *American Foundations: An Investigative History*. Cambridge, MA: MIT Press, 2002.

Katherine Fulton and Andrew Blau. *Looking Out for the Future: An Orientation for Twenty-First Century Philanthropists*. Cambridge, MA: Monitor Company Group, 2005. (available at www.futureofphilanthropy.org)

Emmett D. Carson. "The Seven Deadly Myths of the U.S. Nonprofit Sector: Implications for Promoting Social Justice Worldwide." In *Beyond Racism: Race and Inequality in Brazil, South Africa, and the United States*, eds. Charles V. Hamilton et al. Boulder: Lynne Rienner Publishers, 2001.

Ruthie Gilmore and Suzanne Pharr. *Keynotes* from *The Revolution Will Not Be Funded: Beyond The Non-Profit Industrial Complex*, April 30-May 1, 2004. (available at www.incite-national.org).

Peter Karoff, ed. *Just Money: A Critique of Contemporary American Philanthropy*. Boston: TPI Editions, 2004.

Amy Kass, ed. *The Perfect Gift: The Philanthropic Imagination in Poetry and Prose*. Bloomington: Indiana University Press, 2002.

Ellen Condliffe Lagemann, ed. *Philanthropic Foundations: New Scholarship, New Possibilities*. Bloomington: Indiana University Press, 1999.

Michael Lerner. *A Gift Observed: Reflections on Philanthropy and Civilization*. Bolinas: Common Knowledge Press, 2005.

Francie Ostrawer. *Why the Wealthy Give: The Culture of Elite Philanthropy*. Princeton: Princeton University Press, 1995.

Stacy Palmer, ed. *Challenges for Nonprofits and Philanthropy, The Courage to Change: Three Decades of Reflections by Pablo Eisenberg*. Medford, MA: Tufts University Press, 2004.

Michael Porter and Mark Kramer. "Philanthropy's New Agenda: Creating Value." *Harvard Business Review* (November/December 1999): 121-130.

Barry D. Karl and Stanley Katz. "Foundations and Ruling Class Elites." *Daedalus* 116 (Winter 1987): 1-40.

Teresa Odendahl. *Charity Begins at Home: Generosity and Self-Interest Among the Philanthropic Elite*. New York: Basic Books, Inc., 1990.

Rob Reich. "A Failure of Philanthropy: American charity shortchanges the poor, and public policy is partly to blame." *Social Innovation Review* (Winter 2005): 24-33.

Ira Silver. "Buying an activist identity: reproducing class through social movement philanthropy." *Sociological Perspectives* 41, no. 2 (Summer, 1998): 303-321.

Stephen Viederman. "The Future of Philanthropy." *Souls: A Critical Journal of Black Politics, Culture and Society* (Winter 2002).

Kurt Vonnegut. *God Bless You Mr. Rosewater*. New York: Dell Publishing, 1965.

Grantee and activist perspectives on philanthropy

Orson Aguilar et al. *Fairness in Philanthropy Part II: Perspectives from the Field*. Greenling Institute, 2005.

Jeanne Bell et al. *Daring to Lead: 2006, A National Study of Nonprofit Executive Leadership*. CompassPoint Nonprofit Services and The Meyer Foundation, 2006.

Robert O. Bothwell. *Foundation funding of grassroots organizations*. Washington, DC: National Committee for Responsive Philanthropy, 2000.

The Center for Effective Philanthropy. *Listening To Grantees: What Nonprofits Value in Their Foundation Funders*. Cambridge, MA: Center for Effective Philanthropy, 2004.

Publications about social change philanthropy

Emmett D. Carson. "The Role of Indigenous and Institutional Philanthropy in Advancing Social Justice." In *Philanthropy and the Nonprofit Sector in a Changing America*, eds. Charles T. Clotfelter and Thomas Ehrlich. Bloomington: Indiana University Press, 1999.

Changemakers. *Legacy and Innovation: A Guidebook for Families on Social Change Philanthropy*. San Francisco: Changemakers, forthcoming.

Elayne Clift ed. *Women, Philanthropy, and Social Change: Visions for a Just Society*. Hanover, NH: University Press of New England, 2005.

Chuck Collins and Pam Rogers with Joan P. Garner. *Robin Hood Was

Right: A Guide to Giving Your Money for Social Change. New York: W.W. Norton & Company, 2001.

Daniel Farber and Deborah McCarthy, eds. *Foundations for Social Change: Critical Perspectives on Philanthropy and Popular Movements*. Lanham, MD: Rowman & Littlfield Publishers, Inc., 2005.

Alison D. Goldberg. "Social Change Philanthropy and How It's Done." *Foundation News & Commentary* 43, no. 3 (May/June 2002): 36-40.

John Hunsaker and Brenda Hanzl. *Understanding Social Justice Philanthropy*. Washington, DC: National Committee for Responsive Philanthropy, 2003.

Craig Jenkins and Abigail L. Halci. "Grassrooting the System?: The Development and Impact of Social Movement Philanthropy, 1953-1990." In *Philanthropic Foundations: New Scholarship, New Possibilities*, ed. Ellen Condliffe Lagemann. Bloomington: Indiana University Press, 1999.

Michael May. *Are We Ready? Social Change Philanthropy and the Coming $10 Trillion Transfer of Wealth*. Washington, DC: National Committee for Responsive Philanthropy, 1999.

Christopher Mogil and Anne Slepian. *Welcome to Philanthropy: Resources for Individuals and Families Exploring Social Change Giving*. San Diego: National Network of Grantmakers, 1997.

Christopher Mogil and Anne Slepian with Pete Woodrow. *We Gave Away a Fortune*. Gabriola Island, BC: New Society Publishers, 1992.

Anne Firth Murray. *Paradigm Found: Leading and Managing for Positive Change*. Novato, CA: New World Library, 2006.

National Committee for Responsive Philanthropy. *Social Justice Philanthropy: The Latest Trend or a Lasting Lens for Grantmaking?*. Washington, DC: National Committee for Responsive Philanthropy, April 2005.

National Network of Grantmakers. *Grantmakers Directory 2000-2001*. San Diego: National Network of Grantmakers, 2001.

Teresa Odendahl and William A. Diaz. "Independent Foundations in Transition." In *The Meaning and Impact of Board and Staff Diversity in the Philanthropic Field, Findings from a National Study*, ed. Chris Cardona. Joint Affinity Groups, 2002. (available at www.disabilityfunders.org/jagresrch.pdf)

Susan Ostrander. *Money for Change: Social Movement Philanthropy at Haymarket People's Fund.* Philadelphia: Temple University Press, 1997.

Susan A. Ostrander. "When Grantees Become Grantors." In *Philanthropic Foundations: New Scholarship, New Possibilities*, ed. Ellen Condliffe Lagemann. Bloomington: Indiana University Press, 1999.

Alan Rabinowitz. *Social Change Philanthropy in America.* New York: Quorum Books, 1990

Aileen Shaw. *Social Justice Philanthropy: An Overview.* New York: Synergos Institute, *2002.*

Tides Foundation. *Donor Activist Collaboration: A Potential Vehicle for Promoting Community, Accountability and Effectiveness in Grantmaking.* San Francisco: The Tides Foundation, 2003.

Philanthropy journals and newsletters

ASF Quarterly Newsletter, Association of Small Foundations (www.small-foundations.org)

The Chronicle of Philanthropy (www.philanthropy.com)

Family Matters Now, Council on Foundations (www.cof.org)

Family Giving News, National Center for Family Philanthropy (www.ncfp.org)

Foundation News & Commentary, Council on Foundations (www.foundationnews.org)

Philanthropy Journal, www.philanthropyjournal.org

Philanthropy News Digest, Foundation Center (www.foundationcenter.org)

Responsive Philanthropy, National Committee for Responsive Philanthropy (www.ncrp.org)

Stanford Social Innovation Review, Center for Social Innovation, Stanford Graduate School of Business (www.ssir.org)

Philanthropy statistics

Besides philanthropy organizations, a number of other groups track and interpret trends related to giving.

National Center for Charitable Statistics
Center on Nonprofits and Philanthropy, Urban Institute
www.urban.org/center/cnp/index.cfm
(202) 833-7200

Center on Wealth and Philanthropy
Boston College
www.bc.edu/research/swri/
(617) 522-4070

The Foundation Center
www.foundationcenter.org
(212) 620-4230

Giving Institute
www.givingusa.org
(847) 375-4709

New Tithing Group
www.newtithing.org
(415) 274-2754

Family philanthropy
These organizations provide support to family funds through conferences,
publications, and membership services.

Association of Small Foundations
www.smallfoundations.org
(301) 907-3337

Council on Foundations
www.cof.org
(202) 466-6512

Forum of Regional Associations of Grantmakers
www.givingforum.org
(202) 467-1120

National Center on Family Philanthropy
www.ncfp.org
(202) 293-3424

PUBLICATIONS:

Sara Beggs et al., eds. *The New Foundation Guidebook: Building a Strong Foundation*. Washington, DC: Association of Small Foundations, 2003.

Ellen Bryson. *Top Ten Ways Family Foundations Get Into Trouble,* 2nd ed. Washington, DC: Council on Foundations, 2002.

Council on Foundations. *Family Foundation Library Series*. Washington, DC: Council on Foundations, 1997.

John Edie. *First Steps in Starting a Foundation*. Washington, DC: Council on Foundations, 2002.

John Edie. *Family Foundations and the Law: What You Need to Know*. Washington, DC: Council on Foundations, 2002.

Virginia Esposito, ed. *Splendid Legacy: The Guide to Creating Your Family Foundation*. Washington, DC: National Center for Family Philanthropy, 2002.

Elaine Gast. *Built on Principle: A Guide to Family Foundation Stewardship*. Washington, DC: Council on Foundations, 2006.

Kelin Gersick et al. *The Succession Workbook: Continuity for Family Foundations*. Washington, DC: Council on Foundations, 2000.

National Center for Family Philanthropy. *The Trustee Notebook: An Orientation for Family Foundation Board Members*. Washington, DC: National Center for Family Philanthropy, 1999.

WEB RESOURCES

Association of Small Foundations, *Foundation in a Box*, www.foundationinabox.org

Council on Foundations, *Stewardship Principles for Family Foundations*, www.cof.org

National Center for Family Philanthropy, *Family Philanthropy Online*, www.ncfp.org

Intergenerational philanthropy

Council on Michigan Foundations. *Preparing the Next Generations: A Workbook of Practical Ideas and Activities to Foster Intergenerational Involvement in Family Foundations*. Grand Haven, MI: Council of Michigan Foundations, 2001.

Virginia Esposito. *Successful Succession: Inspiring and Preparing a Next Generation of Charitable Leaders*. Washington, DC: National Center for Family Philanthropy, 2003.

Kelin Gersick. *Generations of Giving*. Washington, DC: National Center for Family Philanthropy, 2004.

Alison D. Goldberg. *Opportunity of a Lifetime: Young Adults in Family Philanthropy*. Washington, DC: National Center for Family Philanthropy, 2002.

Sharna Goldseker. "Beyond Duty and Obligation." *Foundation News & Commentary* 47, no. 1 (January/February 2006).

Susan Crites Price. *The Giving Family: Raising Our Children to Help Others*. Washington, DC: Council on Foundations, 2000.

Young people in philanthropy organizations

21/64, Andrea and Charles Bronfman Philanthropies
www.2164.net
(212) 931-0109
Consults with families, foundations, and
individuals on generational transition.

Emerging Practitioners in Philanthropy
www.epip.org
(212) 472-0508
A network of young and emerging grantmakers who are
interested in advancing effective social justice philanthropy.

Learning To Give
www.learningtogive.org
(231) 767-1780
Offers lessons, plans, activities, and resources to
educate youth about philanthropy.

Younger Funders Group, Jewish Funders Network
www.jfunders.org
(212) 726-0177

Youth Give
www.youthgive.org
(415) 388-1222
Creates tools and programs to enable children, youth,
and families to learn, engage, and give.

Youth Leadership Institute
www.yli.org
(415) 836-9160
Designs community-based youth grantmaking programs.

Social change philanthropy organizations and affinity groups
Asian Americans/Pacific Islanders in Philanthropy (AAPIP)
www.aapip.org
(415) 273-2760

Association of Black Foundation Executives (ABFE)
www.abfe.org
(212) 982.6925 x510

Changemakers
www.changemakers.org
(415) 551-2363
A national public foundation that models and supports community-based social change philanthropy.

Disability Funders Network
www.disabilityfunders.org
(703) 560-0099

Emerging Practitioners in Philanthropy (EPIP)
www.epip.org
(212) 472-0508

Environmental Grantmakers Association
www.ega.org
(212) 812-4260

Funders for Lesbian and Gay Issues
www.lgbtfunders.org
(212) 475-2930

Funders Network on Trade and Globalization
www.fntg.org
(415) 642-6022

Grantmakers Concerned with Immigrants and Refugees
www.gcir.org
(707) 824-4374

Grantmakers Without Borders

www.internationaldonors.org

(617) 794-2253

A network of foundations and donors committed to expanding global social change philanthropy.

Hispanics in Philanthropy

www.hiponline.org

(415) 837-0427

National Committee for Responsive Philanthropy (NCRP)

www.ncrp.org

(202) 387-9177

A national watchdog, research, and advocacy organization that promotes public accountability and accessibility in philanthropy.

National Network of Grantmakers (NNG)

www.nng.org

(612) 724-0702

NNG is a membership network of foundations and individuals involved in funding social and economic justice.

Native Americans in Philanthropy

www.nativephilanthropy.org

(612) 724-8798

Neighborhood Funders Group

www.nfg.org

(202) 833-4690

A network of funders that support community-based efforts that improve economic and social conditions in low-income communities.

Racial Justice Collaborative

www.racialjusticecollaborative.org

(212) 764-1508 x216

Tides Foundation

www.tides.org

(415) 561-6400

Partners with donors to increase and organize resources for positive social change.

Twenty-First Century Foundation

www.21cf.org

(212) 662-3700

A national foundation that supports African-American community revitalization, education, and leadership development.

Women & Philanthropy

www.womenphil.org

(877) 293-8809

An association of grantmakers dedicated to achieving equity for women and girls.

Women's Funding Network

www.wfnet.org

(415) 441-0706

A membership organization of more than ninety public and private women's foundations that empower women and girls.

Activist-led funds

These sites also have extensive lists of activist led funds: www.changemakers.org, www.fex.org, and www.wfnet.org.

Astraea Lesbian Action Foundation

www.astraea.org

(212) 529-8021

The Funding Exchange

www.fex.org

(212) 529-5300

A network of social justice community funds across the country.

Global Fund for Women

www.globalfundforwomen.org

(415) 202-7640

Global Greengrants Fund

www.greengrants.org

(303) 939-9866

International Development Exchange

www.idex.org

(415) 824-8384

Jewish Funds for Justice
www.shefafund.org
(212) 213-2113

Ms. Foundation
www.ms.foundation.org
(212) 742-2300

The New World Foundation
www.newwf.org
(212) 249-1023
Grants to strengthen and expand civil rights and active
participation in democracy.

Peace Development Fund
www.peacefund.org
(413) 256-8306

RESIST, Inc.
www.resistinc.org
(617) 623-5110

Southern Partners Fund
www.spfund.org
(404) 758-1983

Third Wave Foundation
www.thirdwavefoundation.org
(212) 675-0700
Supports the leadership of young women and transgender youth.

People of color in philanthropy

In addition to many of the organizations listed in "Social change philanthropy organizations," these groups provide resources to people of color in
philanthropy:

The Coalition for New Philanthropy
www.nyrag.org/coalition
(212) 924-6744
Initiative to promote philanthropy in the African-American, Latino, and
Asian-American communities throughout metropolitan New York.

National Black United Fund
www.nbuf.org
(973) 643-5122
Uses philanthropic resources to meet vital needs in Black communities.

National Center for Black Philanthropy
www.ncfbp.net
(202) 530-9770

Twenty-First Century Foundation
www.21cf.org
(212) 662-3700

Ujamaa
Grassroots Leadership
www.grassrootsleadership.org
(704) 332-3090 x14

PUBLICATIONS:

Felinda Mottino and Eugene D. Miller. *Pathways for Change: Philanthropy Among African American, Asian American, and Latino Donors in the New York Metropolitan Region*. New York: Center on Philanthropy and Civil Society at The Graduate Center, The City University of New York and the Coalition for New Philanthropy, 2004.

Council on Foundations. *Cultures of Caring: Philanthropy in Diverse American Communities*. Washington, DC: Council on Foundations, 1999.

James A. Joseph. *Remaking America: How the Benevolent Traditions of Many Cultures Are Transforming Our National Life*. San Francisco: Jossey-Bass, 1995.

Bradford Smith et al. *Philanthropy in Communities of Color*. Bloomington: Indiana University Press, 1999.

Lisa Sullivan. "The New Black Millionaires and Black Philanthropy in the 21st Century." *Responsive Philanthropy* (Fall 2000).

Inequality

Chuck Collins, Scott Klinger and Mike Lapham. *I Didn't Do It Alone: Society's Contribution to Individual Wealth and Success*. Boston, MA: United for a Fair Economy and Responsible Wealth, 2004.

Chuck Collins and Felice Yeskel with United for a Fair Economy and Class Action. *Economic Apartheid in America: a Primer on Economic Inequality and Insecurity*. New York: New Press, 2005.

Dollars & Sense and United for a Fair Economy, eds. *The Wealth Inequality Reader*. Cambridge, MA: Dollars & Sense, 2004.

William H. Gates, Sr. and Chuck Collins. *Wealth and Our Commonwealth: Why America Should Tax Accumulated Fortunes*. Boston: Beacon Press, 2002.

John Havens and Paul Schervish. *Millionaires and the Millennium: New Estimates of the Forthcoming Wealth Transfer and the Prospects for a Golden Age of Philanthropy*. Boston: Boston College Social Welfare Research Institute, 1999.

David Cay Johnston. *Perfectly Legal: The Covert Campaign to Rig Our Tax System to Benefit the Super Rich—and Cheat Everybody Else*. New York: Penguin, 2003.

Meizhu Lui et al. *The Color of Wealth: The Story Behind the U.S. Racial Wealth Divide*. Boston: United for a Fair Economy, 2006.

Melvin L. Oliver and Thomas M. Shapiro. *Black Wealth, White Wealth: A New Perspective on Racial Inequality*. New York: Routledge, 1997.

Sam Pizzigati. *Greed and Good: Understanding and Overcoming the Inequality That Limits Our Lives*. New York: Apex Press, 2004.

United Nations Development Programme. *Human Development Report 2005: International cooperation at a crossroads. Aid, trade, and security in an unequal world*. New York: United Nations Development Programme, 2005.

Social change movements

Here's a starter list adapted from the Movement Strategy Center (see www.movementstrategy.org for more extensive resources):

John Anner, ed. *Beyond Identity Politics: Emerging Social Justice Movements in Communities of Color*. Boston: South End Press, 1996.

Marcy Darnovsky et al. *Cultural Politics and Social Movements*. Philadelphia: Temple University Press, 1995.

Bill Moyer. *Doing Democracy: The MAP Model for Organizing Social Movements*. Philadelphia: New Society Publishers, 2001.

David Solnit, ed. *Globalize Liberation: How to Uproot the System and Build a Better World*. San Francisco: City Lights Press, 2004.

Jervis Anderson. *Bayard Rustin: Troubles I've Seen*. Berkeley: University of California Press, 1998.

Ponna Wignaraja, ed. *New Social Movements in the South: Empowering the People*. London: Zed Books, 1993.

Howard Zinn. *A People's History of the United States: 1492-Present*. New York: HarperCollins, 2005.

Grantmaking

In addition to workshops offered by family philanthropy organizations, the following groups provide grantmaking training:

Philanthropology Workshops, Emerging Practitioners in Philanthropy
www.epip.org
(212) 497-7547
Grantmaker education program provides EPIP members with
peer-based and intergenerational professional development.

Grantcraft, The Ford Foundation
www.grantcraft.org
Distills the practical wisdom of grantmakers into
guides, videos, workshops, and other tools.
(212) 573-4879

The Grantmaking School, Grand Valley State University
www.grantmakingschool.org
(616) 331-7589
A university-based program for teaching the techniques and ethics of grantmaking specifically to foundation grantmaking professionals.

The Philanthropy Workshop, The Rockefeller Foundation
www.rockfound.org
(212) 869-8500
A leadership development and networking program for individual donors who wish to bring their philanthropy to a more strategic level.

PUBLICATIONS:
Alliance for Justice. *Build Your Advocacy Grantmaking*. Washington, DC: Alliance for Justice, 2005.

Alliance for Justice. *Investing in Change: A Funder's Guide to Supporting Advocacy*. Washington, DC: Alliance for Justice, 2004.

Tracy Gary and Melissa Kohner. *Inspired Philanthropy: Your Step-By-Step Guide to Creating a Giving Plan*. San Francisco: Chardon Press, 2002.

Barbara Kibbe et al. *Grantmaking Basics: A Field Guide for Funders*. Washington, DC: Council on Foundations, 2005.

Ellen Furnari, Carol Mollner, Teresa Odendahl and Aileen Shaw. *Exemplary Grantmaking Practices Manual*. San Francisco: National Network of Grantmakers, 1997.

Independent Sector. *Guidelines for the Funding of Nonprofit Organizations*. www.independentsector.org.

Kay Sprinkle Grace. *High Impact Philanthropy: How Donors, Boards, and Nonprofit Organizations Can Transform Communities*. New York: John Wiley & Sons, 2001.

Grantmakers without Borders. *International Grantmaking Resource Packet*. (Available at www.internationaldonors.org, which also includes links to other international grantmaking resources.)

Joel Orosz. *The Insider's Guide to Grantmaking: How Foundations Find, Fund, and Manage Effective Programs*. San Francisco: Jossey Bass, 2000.

Larry Parachini and Sally Convington. *Community Organizing Toolbox: A Funder's Guide to Community Organizing*. Washington, DC: Neighborhood Funders Group, 2001. (available at www.nfg.org)

Fred Setterberg et al. *Grantmaking Basics II: A Field Guide for Funders*. Washington, DC: Council on Foundations, 2004.

Non-profit databases

These searchable databases provide information about non-profit groups:

Action without Borders
www.idealist.org

Charity Navigator
www.charitynavigator.org

Guidestar
www.guidestar.org

Board development

Boardsource
www.boardsource.org
(202) 452-6262

Youth on Board
www.youthonboard.org
(617) 623-9900 x1242

Youth Leadership Institute
www.yli.org
(415) 836-9160

Training in facilitation
Public Conversations Project
www.publicconversations.org
(617) 923-1216
Promotes constructive conversations and relationships among people who have differing values, world views and perspectives about divisive public issues.

National Coalition for Dialogue and Deliberation
www.thataway.org
(802) 254-7341
Brings together those who actively practice, promote, and study inclusive, high quality conversations.

Interaction Institute for Social Change
www.interactioninstitute.org
(617) 234-2750
Provides individuals with the skills they need to develop personally and professionally catalysts for improving performance, building collaborative cultures, and achieving extraordinary results.

Rockwood Leadership Program
www.rockwoodfund.org
Provides leadership trainings across the country for people involved in social change.

PUBLICATIONS:
Elaine Gast. *Principled Planning: A Guide for Family Foundation Retreats.* Washington, DC: Council on Foundations, 2006.

Finding philanthropic advisors and facilitators

In addition to seeking referrals from family philanthropy organizations, these groups may be helpful:

National Network of Consultants to Grantmakers
www.nncg.org
(888) 589-4489

Inspired Legacies
www.inspiredlegacies.com
(713) 527-7671
Provides support on legacy, financial, and philanthropic planning.

Diversity and inclusiveness resources for funders

Contact the Philanthropic Initiative for Racial Equity (www.racialequity.org) for a comprehensive resource list.

Orson Aguilar et al. *Fairness in Philanthropy, Part I: Foundation Giving to Minority-led Nonprofits*. Berkeley: Greenlining Institute, November 2005. (available at www.greenlining.org)

Applied Research Center and Philanthropic Initiative for Racial Equity. *Racial Justice Grantmaking Assessment Tool*. Washington, DC: Philanthropic Initiative for Racial Equity, forthcoming.

Zita Arocha. *Inclusiveness and Family Foundations*. Washington, DC: Council on Foundations, 1993.

Mary Ellen S. Capek and Molly Mead. *Effective Philanthropy: Organizational Success Through Deep Diversity and Gender Equality*. Cambridge, MA: MIT Press, 2006.

Chris Cardona, ed. *The Meaning and Impact of Board and Staff Diversity in the Philanthropic Field, Findings from a National Study*. Joint Affinity Groups, 2002. (available at www.disabilityfunders.org/jagresrch.pdf)

Disability Funders Network. *A Screening Tool for Disability-Inclusive Grantmaking*. Falls Church, VA: Disability Funders Network. (available at www.disabilityfunders.org)

Donors Forum of Chicago et al. *Building on a Better Foundation: A Toolkit for Creating an Inclusive Grantmaking Organization*. Donors Forum of Chicago et al, 2001. (available at www.mcf.org)

Jean E. Fairfax. "For Times Like These; More Black Trustees." James A. Joseph Lecture on Philanthropy, 1996. (available at www.abfe.org; also, see the other lectures on the site)

Marcia Festen et al. *ClearSighted: A Grantmaker's Guide to Using a Gender Lens*. Chicago: Chicago Women in Philanthropy, 1996. (available at www.cwiponline.org)

Funders for Lesbian and Gay Issues. *Expanding Opportunities: A Grantmaker's Guide to Workplace Policies for Lesbian, Gay and Bisexual Staff*. New York: Funders for Lesbian and Gay Issues, 2002.

Funders for Lesbian and Gay Issues. *The Grantmakers's Guide to Lesbian, Gay, Bisexual and Transgender Issues*. New York: Funders for Lesbian and Gay Issues.

GrantCraft/Philanthropic Initiative for Racial Equity. *Guide to Grantmaking with a Racial Equity Lens*. Washington, DC: GrantCraft, forthcoming.

Handy Lindsey, Jr. "Philanthropy's Record on Diversity and Inclusiveness: An Inconvenient Truth." James A. Joseph Lecture on Philanthropy, 2003.

Steven Mayer et al. *Moving Philanthropy Closer to Racial Equity and Social Justice: Working Drafts of Tools For Making Further Progress*. Minneapolis: Effective Communities LLC, March 2006. (available at www.effectivecommunities.com)

Will Pittz and Rinku Sen. *Short Changed: Foundation Giving and Communities of Color*. Oakland: Applied Research Center, 2004.

Sheila Romero. *The Honest Truth: Lessons Learned from the Stories of People of Color in Philanthropy*. Minneapolis: National Network of Grantmakers, Native Americans in Philanthropy, and Wilder Research, 2006.

Jeri Spann. *The Value of Difference: Enhancing Philanthropy Through Inclusiveness in Governance, Staffing and Grantmaking*. Washington, DC: Council on Foundations, 1993.

Bernard C. Watson. "Minorities and Marginality in American Foundations." James A. Joseph Lecture on Philanthropy, 1993.

Western States Center. *Dismantling Racism: A Resource Book*. Portland, OR: Western States Center, 2003. (available at www.westernstatescenter.org)

Anti-oppression organizations
Applied Research Center
www.arc.org

(510) 653-3415

A public policy, educational and research institute whose work emphasizes issues of race and social change. They also publish *Colorlines Magazine*, the nation's leading magazine on race, culture, and organizing.

Class Action
www.classism.org

(413) 585-9709

Class Action focuses on the personal, interpersonal, and organizational levels of classism. They serve as a national resource center on class, providing individuals and organizations with the tools and resources to work on eliminating classism.

Challenging White Supremacy Workshop
www.cwsworkshop.org

(415) 647-0921

Committed to helping white social justice activists become principled and effective anti-racist organizers—both to challenge white privilege and to work for racial justice in all social justice work.

The Mandala Center
www.mandalaforchange.com

(360) 344-3435

A multi-disciplinary education organization dedicated to community dialogue, social justice and personal transformation.

National Women's Alliance
www.nwaforchange.org

(202) 518-5411

A community-driven national advocacy organization dedicated to ending all forms of oppression against women and girls of color.

National Youth Advocacy Coalition
www.nyacyouth.org

(202) 319-7596

A social justice organization that advocates for and with young people who are lesbian, gay, bisexual, transgender or questioning (LGBTQ) in an effort to end discrimination against these youth and to ensure their physical and emotional well being.

The People's Institute for Survival and Beyond
www.thepeoplesinstitute.org
(504) 241-7472
Dedicated to examining history, culture, internal dynamics of leadership
and networking to help others face the issue of racism and learn to
educate others for twenty-three years.

SOUL
www.youthec.org/soul/
(510) 451-5466
A training center to develop a new multi-racial generation of young
organizers who will have the skills and the vision they need to struggle
for the liberation of all oppressed people.

Training for Change
www.trainingforchange.org
(215) 241-7035
Dedicated to helping groups stand up for justice, peace, and
the environment through strategic non-violence.

Western States Center
www.westernstatescenter.org
(503) 228-8866
Works to build a progressive movement for social, economic, racial, and
environmental justice in the eight western states of Oregon, Washington,
Idaho, Montana, Wyoming, Utah, Nevada, and Alaska.

Cross-class collaboration

bell hooks. *Where We Stand: Class Matters*. New York: Routledge, 2000.

Betsy Leondar-Wright. *Class Matters: Cross-Class Alliance Building for
Middle-Class Activists*. Gabriola Island, BC: New Society Publishers, 2005.
(Also see the companion website, www.classmatters.org.)

Fred Rose. *Coalitions across the Class Divide*. Ithaca, NY: Cornell
University, 2000.

Linda Stout. *Bridging the Class Divide and Other Lessons from Grassroots
Organizing*. Boston: Beacon Press, 1997.

Financial literacy
Investor Words
www.investorwords.com
A big investment glossary.

My Money
www.mymoney.gov
A helpful financial literacy site.

The Motley Fool
www.fool.com
This site has some pretty easy to read explanations of how financial planning and investing work.

Socially responsible investing
As You Sow
www.asyousow.org
(415) 391-3212
A non-profit organization dedicated to promoting corporate social responsibility.

CERES
www.ceres.org
(617) 247-0700
A national network of investment funds, environmental organizations and other public interest groups working to advance environmental stewardship on the part of businesses.

Community Development Finance Institutions Coalition
www.cdfi.org
(703) 294-6970

Corpwatch
www.corpwatch.org
(510) 271-8080

CorpWatch counters corporate-led globalization through education, network-building, and activism.

First Affirmative Financial Network

www.firstaffirmative.com

(800) 422-7284

An independent advisory firm that supports a nationwide network of financial advisors specializing in a socially responsible approach to investing.

Foundation Partnership on Corporate Responsibility

www.foundationpartnership.org

An association of foundations working to link their grantmaking values with their investments.

Green Money Journal

www.greenmoney.org

(505) 988-7423

Focuses on socially and environmentally responsible business, investing, and consumer resources.

Interfaith Center on Corporate Responsibility

www.iccr.org

(212) 870-2293

An association of faith-based members that press companies to be socially and environmentally responsible.

Investor's Circle

www.investorscircle.net

(617) 566-2600

A social venture capital intermediary whose mission is to support early-stage, private companies that drive the transition to a sustainable economy.

Jessie Smith Noyes Foundation

www.noyes.org

(212) 684-6577

A private foundation that has documented its experience with SRI.

National Community Capital Association

www.communitycapital.org

(215) 923-4754

National Federation of Community Development Credit Unions

www.natfed.org

(212) 809-1850

Social Funds

www.socialfunds.com

Has information on SRI mutual funds, community investments, corporate research, shareowner actions, and daily social investment news.

Social Investment Forum

www.socialinvest.org

www.communityinvesting.org

A national non-profit organization providing research and educational programs on SRI.

Responsible Endowments Coalition

www.sriendowment.org

A diverse network of students and alumni from across the country dedicated to advancing socially and environmentally responsible investing in relation to college and university endowments.

Responsible Investing

www.responsibleinvesting.org

A public database containing complete equity holdings and screening categories of SRI mutual funds in the United States and Canada.

Responsible Wealth

www.responsiblewealth.org

(617) 423-2148

A national network of businesspeople, investors and affluent Americans who are concerned about deepening economic inequality and are working for widespread prosperity.

PUBLICATIONS:

Hal Brill. *Investing with Your Values: Making Money and Making a Difference.* Princeton: Bloomberg Press, 2000.

Peter Camejo. *The SRI Advantage: Why Socially Responsible Investing Has Outperformed Financially.* Gabriola Island, BC: New Society Publishers, 2002.

Rick Cohen. *A Call for Mission-Based Investing by America's Private Foundations.* Washington, DC: National Committee for Responsive Philanthropy, 2005.

Harriet Denison. "There's much more we can do." *Foundation News & Commentary* 42 no. 1 (January/February 2001).

Amy L. Domini. *Socially Responsible Investing: Making a Difference and Making Money*. Chicago: Dearborn Trade, 2001.

Jed Emerson. "Where Money Meets Mission: Breaking Down the Firewall Between Foundation Investments and Programming." *Stanford Social Innovation Review*, (Summer 2003): 38-47.

Ben Gose. "A Focus on Corporate Responsibility." *Chronicle on Philanthropy* 7:20 (2005).

John C. Harrington. *The Challenge to Power: Money, Investing, and Democracy*. White River Junction, VT: Chelsea Green Publishing Company, 2005.

Rockefeller Philanthropy Advisors and As You Sow Foundation. *Unlocking the Power of the Proxy: How Active Foundation Proxy Voting Can Protect Endowments and Boost Philanthropic Missions*. New York: Rockefeller Philanthropy Advisors, 2004.

Socially responsible spending and business practices

Business Alliance for Local Living Economies

www.livingeconomies.org

(415) 255-1108

An international alliance of independently operated local business networks dedicated to building local living economies.

Businesses for Social Responsibility

www.bsr.org

(415) 984-3200

A global organization that helps member companies achieve success in ways that respect ethical values, people, communities, and the environment.

Co-op America

www.coopamerica.org

(800) 584-7336

A national nonprofit organization that provides practical steps for leveraging consumer and investor resources for social change.

Fair Trade Federation

www.fairtradefederation.org

(202) 872-5338

An association of fair trade wholesalers, retailers, and producers. Includes a directory of members' stores and on-line shopping sites.

Green Pages

www.greenpages.org

(800) 584-7336

Directory of qualified green businesses with over 25,000 products and services from 2,000 green companies.

Social Venture Network

www.svn.org

(415) 561-6501

A progressive business network that offers support for companies that value social justice, community, cooperation, diversity, education, sustainability, and innovation.

Union Label

www.unionlabel.org

Promotes the products and services produced in America by union members.

PUBLICATIONS:

Michael Brower and Warren Leon. *The Consumer's Guide to Effective Environmental Choices: Practical Advice from the Union of Concerned Scientists.* New York: Three Rivers Press, 1999.

Ingrid Newkirk. *Making Kind Choices: Everyday Ways to Enhance Your Life Through Earth- and Animal-Friendly Living.* New York: St. Martin's Griffin, 2005.

John Robbins. *Diet for a New America: How Your Food Choices Affect Your Health, Happiness and the Future of Life on Earth.* Tiburon, CA: H.J. Kramer, 1998.

Payout

Thomas Billitteri. "Money, Mission, and the Payout Rule: In Search of a Strategic Approach to Foundation Spending." *Nonprofit Sector Research Fund Working Paper Series*, Aspen Institute (June 2005).

Elaine Gast. *Facing Forever: Planning for Change in Family Foundations.* Washington, DC: Council on Foundations, 2004.

Jeff Krehely. "Saying 'No' to Forever: Why Some Foundations Spend Down." *Responsive Philanthropy* (Spring 2004).

Fundraising

Changemakers Donor Partner Training

www.changemakers.org/donorprograms.htm

(415) 551-2363

Changemakers works with committed social change donors to foster and advance their leadership, partnership, and fundraising skills.

Grassroots Fundraising Journal

www.grassrootsfundraising.org

Offers practical tips and tools to help with raising money for organizations.

Grassroots Institute for Fundraising Training (GIFT)

www.grassrootsinstitute.org

(303) 455-6361

GIFT's mission is to change the color of philanthropy by developing and strengthening the grassroots fundraising skills of individuals and organizations working for social justice, with an emphasis on communities of color.

PUBLICATIONS:

Kim Klein, *Fundraising for Social Change.* San Francisco: Jossey-Bass, 2000.

Resist, *Finding Funding: A Beginner's Guide to Foundation Research,* 5th ed. (available at www.resistinc.org/resources/finding_funding.html)

Alison Goldberg joined Resource Generation's staff after the organization she created and directed, Foundations for Change, merged with RG. She has worked for a number of non-profits and within her own family's foundation to promote social and economic justice. Her previous publications include "Opportunity of a Lifetime: Young Adults in Family Philanthropy" for the National Center for Family Philanthropy's *Passages Series* and "Social Change Philanthropy and How It's Done" for *Foundation News & Commentary*. She's 32 and lives in the Boston area.

Karen Pittelman is the author of Resource Generation's *Classified: How to Stop Hiding Your Privilege and Use It For Social Change* from Soft Skull Press and served as RG's first program coordinator. At 25 she dissolved her $3 million trust fund to co-found the Chahara Foundation, a fund run by and for low-income women activists in Boston. She's now 31 and lives in New York City.

Resource Generation is a national non-profit organization that works with young people with financial wealth who believe in social change. Since 1996, the organization has offered a variety of programs educating young funders about social change philanthropy. RG is located in New York City and led by a cross-class board and staff. You can find out more at www.resourcegeneration.org

Preface

[1] This work was initiated by Foundations for Change, a new organization focused on bringing social change philanthropy into family foundations. As RG's work in this area broadened, the two organizations were able to merge under the umbrella of RG.

[2] This statistic is based on family foundation giving in 2004. The Foundation Center, "Key Facts on Family Foundations, January 2006," http://foundationcenter.org/gainknowledge/research/pdf/key_facts_fam.pdf.

Introduction

[3] Throughout the book "family fund" refers to any type of family giving vehicle, whether a foundation, charitable trust, donor-advised fund, or another entity.

[4] This statistic is based on family foundation giving in 2004. The Foundation Center, "Key Facts."

[5] National Network of Grantmakers, "Social Change Grantmaking in the United States," 1998, http://www.nng.org/html/ourprograms/research/socchangeppr_table.htm.

[6] For a more in-depth discussion about funding social change, see Chuck Collins and Pam Rogers with Joan Garner, *Robin Hood Was Right: A Guide to Giving Your Money For Social Change* (New York: W.W. Norton & Company, 2001).

[7] Chuck Collins and Felice Yeskel with United for a Fair Economy and Class Action, *Economic Apartheid in America: a Primer on Economic Inequality and Insecurity* (New York: New Press, [2000] 2005).

[8] United Nations Development Programme, *Human Development Report 2005: International cooperation at a crossroads. Aid, trade, and security in an unequal world* (New York: United Nations Development Programme, 2005).

Chapter 1

[9] The Merriam-Webster Dictionary defines philanthropy as "goodwill to fellowmen; active effort to promote human welfare." *Merriam-Webster Unabridged Dictionary*, www.m-w.com. See the Resource Section for publications that offer a variety of perspectives on what philanthropy means.

[10] John A. Edie, *Family Foundations and the Law: What You Need To Know*, 3rd ed. (Washington, DC: Council on Foundations, 2005). This estimate is for an unstaffed foundation.

[11] For example, in order to attend a conference at the Council on Foundations, a fund must demonstrate giving in excess of $25,000 each year.

[12] This chapter only scratches the surface of a very complicated history. See the Resource Section to read more about philanthropy's past.

[13] Throughout history there have been numerous examples—especially in our tax policies—where wealthy people receive special opportunities for making and saving money that just aren't available to people who don't have wealth. Many of these policies exist today. See Rob Reich, "A Failure of Philanthropy: American charity shortchanges the poor, and public policy is partly to blame," *Social Innovation Review* (Winter 2005): 24-33 and David Cay Johnston, *Perfectly Legal: The Covert Campaign to Rig Our Tax System to Benefit the Super Rich—and Cheat Everybody Else* (New York: Penguin, 2003).

[14] Estimates from 1912 as cited in William H. Gates, Sr. and Chuck Collins, *Wealth and Our Commonwealth: Why America Should Tax Accumulated Fortunes* (Boston: Beacon Press, 2002), 15.

[15] For examples, see William H. Gates, Sr. and Chuck Collins, *Wealth and Our Commonwealth: Why America Should Tax Accumulated Fortunes* (Boston: Beacon Press, 2002), 37; Richard Magat, *Unlikely Partners: Philanthropic Foundations and the Labor Movement* (Ithaca, NY: Cornell University Press, 1999), 33; Howard Zinn, *A People's History of the United States: 1492-Present* (New York: HarperCollins, [1980] 2005), 276-277 and 354-357.

[16] See www.cof.org for information about this new law, also referred to as "H.R. 4."

[17] The public actually makes a financial contribution to the family in the form of tax relief. Kelin Gersick, *Generations of Giving* (Washington, DC: National Center for Family Philanthropy, 2004), 88.

Chapter 2

[18] Social change philanthropy is also sometimes called "social justice philanthropy" and "community-based philanthropy." For more on this history, see Chuck Collins et al., *Robin Hood Was Right*.

[19] A public foundation is a type of fund that raises money from many people in order to give.

[20] See Rick Cohen, *Community-Based Public Foundations: Small Beacons For Big Ideas* (Washington, DC: National Committee for Responsive Philanthropy, 2004).

[21] See Alan Rabinowitz, *Social Change Philanthropy in America* (New York: Quorum Books, 1990) and Susan A. Ostrander, "When Grantees Become Grantors," in Ellen Condliffe Lagemann, ed., *Philanthropic Foundations: New*

Scholarship, New Possibilities (Bloomington: Indiana University Press, 1999).

[22] From www.weiboldtfoundation.org

[23] See Alan Rabinowitz, *Social Change Philanthropy in America* (New York: Quorum Books, 1990).

[24] See www.generalservice.org and www.needmorfund.org for more information about these funds.

[25] See www.newwf.org.

[26] See www.spfund.org.

Chapter 3

[27] Steven Lawrence, *Family Foundations: A Profile of Funders and Trends* (New York: Foundation Center and National Center for Family Philanthropy, 2000).

[28] For additional reading about inequality and why it's such an important topic to address, see the Resource Section.

[29] Foundation Center, *Foundation Giving Trends: Update on Funding Priorities* (New York: Foundation Center, 2006).

[30] For a discussion about these statistics, see Rob Reich, "A Failure of Philanthropy: American charity shortchanges the poor, and public policy is partly to blame," *Social Innovation Review* (Winter 2005).

[31] Meizhu Lui et al., *The Color of Wealth: The Story Behind the U.S. Racial Wealth Divide* (Boston: United for a Fair Economy, 2006).

[32] Joint Affinity Groups, *Diversity Practices in Foundations: Findings from a National Study* (Joint Affinity Groups, 2001).

[33] For more on this topic, see Teresa Odendahl, *Charity Begins at Home: Generosity and Self-Interest Among the Philanthropic Elite* (New York: Basic Books, Inc., 1990).

[34] During the past thirty years, a group of family funds have been dedicated to furthering a conservative social and political agenda. See Jeff Krehely, Meaghan House and Emily Kernan, *Axis of Ideology: Conservative Foundations and Public Policy* (Washington, DC: National Committee for Responsive Philanthropy, 2004).

[35] Tokenism is when a limited number of people from a group that experiences discrimination are chosen for prestigious positions to deflect criticisms of discrimination. This definition is adapted from the Western States Center, *Dismantling Racism Project*, www.westernstatescenter.org.

[36] Since 1990, general operating support grants have constituted only 12-14 per-cent of total foundation giving. From Jeff Krehely and Meaghan House, *Not All Grants Are Created Equal: Why Nonprofits Need General Operating Support From Foundations* (Washington, DC: National Committee For Responsive Philanthropy, 2005).

[37] For a discussion about the fundraising challenges non-profit directors face, see Jeanne Bell et al., *Daring to Lead: 2006, A National Study of Nonprofit Executive Leadership* (CompassPoint Nonprofit Services and The Meyer Foundation, 2006).

Chapter 5

[38] The Foundation Center, "Key Facts."

[39] See the Appendix for details about how foundations, trusts, and donor-advised funds work.

[40] See Jed Emerson, "Where Money Meets Mission: Breaking Down the Firewall Between Foundation Investments and Programming," *Stanford Social Innovation Review*, (Summer 2003): 38-47.

[41] When the focus of investments is shaped by a fund's mission, SRI is also referred to as Mission-Related or Mission-Based Investing. Some funds also use a strategy called Program-Related Investing, which allows them to count invest-ments toward their qualifying distribution (see "The Foundation Rulebook" for more on this term).

[42] Stockholders of a company receive proxy statements asking for their vote on current resolutions and governances issues.

[43] See Rick Cohen, *A Call for Mission-Based Investing by America's Private Foundations* (Washington, DC: National Committee for Responsive Philanthropy, 2005).

[44] See www.weedenfdn.org.

[45] See www.nathancummings.org.

[46] See www.noyes.org. Also see John C. Harrington, *The Challenge to Power: Money, Investing, and Democracy* (White River Junction, VT: Chelsea Green Publishing Company, 2005).

[47] Karen Labenski and Judith Kroll, *Investment Performance and Practices of Private Foundations* (Washington, DC: Council on Foundations, 2006).

[48] Ben Gose, "A Focus on Corporate Responsibility," *Chronicle on Philanthropy* 7:20 (2005).

[49] Peter Camejo, *The SRI Advantage: Why Socially Responsible Investing Has Outperformed Financially*. Gabriola Island, BC: New Society Publishers, 2002.

Chapter 6

[50] See www.adarc.org.

[51] When faced with a major decline in assets, The Needmor Fund asked twenty-six grantees whether the fund should continue giving grants at the current levels or cut back spending in the short-term to protect the endowment. Nearly all those interviewed expressed that The Needmor Fund should continue its support of community organizing and social change for the long term. The complete account is posted on the Council on Foundations Stewardship Principles and Practices database, www.cof.org.

Chapter 7

[52] See www.cof.org for reports on foundation compensation.

[53] Adapted from a worksheet created by Allen Hancock.

[54] For more discussion on these topics, see Karen Pittelman and Resource Generation, *Classified: How to Stop Hiding Your Privilege and Use it for Social Change* (New York: Soft Skull Press, 2006) and Chuck Collins, Scott Klinger and Mike Lapham, *I Didn't Do It Alone: Society's Contribution to Individual Wealth and Success* (Boston: United for a Fair Economy and Responsible Wealth, 2004).

Chapter 8

[55] Kelin Gersick has written extensively on this topic. See www.lgassoc.com for articles.

[56] This is sometimes called a "bike rack."

Chapter 10

[57] For resources, see Chuck Collins et al., *Robin Hood Was Right*.

[58] To purchase values cards, see www.2164.net. Find additional exercises in Tracy Gary and Melissa Kohner, *Inspired Philanthropy: Your Step-By-Step Guide to Creating a Giving Plan* (San Francisco: Chardon Press, [1998] 2002).

[59] See the Resource Section for sources of philanthropy statistics.

[60] Many activist-led funds and affinity groups run these collaboratives. For example, the Tides Foundation organizes the Bridging the Economic Divide

Initiative in which donors learn about and give to economic justice organizations. See www.tides.org for more information.

[61] For tools on creating a giving plan, see Karen Pittelman and Resource Generation, *Classified*.

Chapter 11

[62] See the Appendix for a description of this term.

Chapter 12

[63] Parts of this list were adapted from Ellen Furnari et al., *Exemplary Grantmaking Practices: Manual* (San Francisco: National Network of Grantmakers, 1997).

[64] See Resource Section for grantee and activist perspectives on philanthropy.

Chapter 13

[65] See bell hooks, *Where We Stand: Class Matters* (New York: Routledge, 2000).

[66] Changemakers and the National Network of Grantmakers can help you locate activist-led funds. Also, see the following publications: Changemakers, *Legacy and Innovation: A Guidebook for Families On Social Change Philanthropy* (San Francisco: Changemakers, forthcoming); Teresa Odendahl and William A. Diaz, "Independent Foundations in Transition," in *The Meaning and Impact of Board and Staff Diversity in the Philanthropic Field, Findings from a National Study*, Chris Cardona, ed. (Joint Affinity Groups, 2002); and Tides Foundation, *Donor Activist Collaboration: A Potential Vehicle for Promoting Community, Accountability and Effectiveness in Grantmaking* (San Francisco: The Tides Foundation, 2003).

[67] See www.hyamsfoundation.org for an example of a foundation diversity policy.

Chapter 14

[68] These questions draw on two resources: Changework, *Dismantling Racism 2002: A Workbook for Social Change Groups* (Changework, 2002) and Donors Forum of Chicago et al., *Building on a Better Foundation: A Toolkit for Creating an Inclusive Grantmaking Organization*, 2001. For more information on anti-racism, diversity, and inclusiveness see the Resource Section.

[69] See Sheila Romero, *The Honest Truth: Lessons Learned from the Stories of People of Color in Philanthropy* (Minneapolis: National Network of Grantmakers, Native Americans in Philanthropy, and Wilder Research, 2006).

[70] These examples are adapted from Tema Okun, "White Supremacy Culture," in *Dismantling Racism 2002: A Workbook for Social Change Groups* (Changework, 2002).

Conclusion

[71] John Havens and Paul Schervish, *Millionaires and the Millennium: New Estimates of the Forthcoming Wealth Transfer and the Prospects for a Golden Age of Philanthropy* (Boston: Boston College Social Welfare Research Institute, 1999).

[72] Chuck Collins and Felice Yeskel with United for a Fair Economy and Class Action, *Economic Apartheid in America: a Primer on Economic Inequality and Insecurity* (New York: New Press, 2005).

Appendix

[73] Infrastructure groups are sometimes also called "intermediary organizations."

[74] Adapted from www.boardsource.org.

[75] See www.cof.org.

[76] These rules were adapted from Association of Small Foundations, *Foundation in a Box*, www.foundationinabox.org; Virginia Esposito, ed., *Splendid Legacy: The Guide To Creating Your Family Foundation* (Washington, DC: National Center for Family Philanthropy, 2002); and National Center for Family Philanthropy, *The Trustee Notebook: An Orientation for Family Foundation Board Members* (Washington, DC: National Center for Family Philanthropy, 1999). The Pension Protection Act of 2006 recently made some important changes to the law that are, at the time of this writing, still being defined. See the "H.R. 4 website" at the Council on Foundations (www.cof.org) or contact their legal department for clarification.

[77] See www.boardsource.org for more information on board member responsibilities.

[78] A foundation has five years from the date when it receives the stock to get rid of the <u>excess business holdings</u>—the amount it owns greater than 20 percent. For more discussion about this rule (and exceptions), see www.irs.gov.

[79] Adapted from *Foundation in a Box*.

[80] "Trustee compensation," the practice of paying foundation board members, is a topic that's been debated in recent years. If your foundation compensates board members, be sure to document that the compensation is both reasonable and necessary to the work of the foundation.

NOTES

NOTES

NOTES